FABER

MARUBA

MARUBA

BY

MAUD MORROW SHARP

Tales of the Mojave Road

Number 10

November 1984

Tales of the Mojave Road
Publishing Company
P.O. Box 307
Norco, California 91760

Library of Congress Catalog Card Number 84-051387
ISBN 0-914224-12-3

Printed by *Rubidoux Printing* of Riverside, California
Binding by *National Bindery* of Pomona, California

for Bert

Caption for picture on preceding page

Bert Sharp and son Jim on *Shrimp* **at Rock Springs Land and Cattle Company Headquarters in Barnwell. The main house is immediately behind them. The small buildings to the right were bunkhouses.**

Maud Sharp Collection

INTRODUCTION

In the space of the past two decades it has become apparent to a growing number of people that the eastern part of the Mojave Desert, referred to as the East Mojave, is the jewel of the California deserts. It is high desert country averaging 2,000 to 5,000 feet elevation with peaks over 7,000 feet and it abounds in natural beauty.

Because of the variation in elevation, it has a tremendous variety of plant life. There are many springs, wells, and wildlife everywhere. The high mountains provide dramatic perspective to wonderful vistas. High sand dunes, impressive lava flows, and concentrations of cinder cones are found in the East Mojave. Also, the most extensive Joshua tree forests in California are there.

The great charm of this country owes its continued existence to the fact that it has remained relatively unknown and unspoiled. Increasing numbers of recreationists are discovering this wonderful land and so far they have brought a high level of sensitivity with them and a recognition that it is necessary to safeguard the values there or they will be lost. Man has touched it--but lightly enough that the signs of his passing are not yet offensive but rather these signs are part of its charm.

There is an impressive inventory of historical remains concentrated in the East Mojave. The mountains and valleys are laced with old Indian trails and wagon roads. Ruins of abandoned mines riddle the hills. Sites of towns long gone and nearly forgotten are numerous, and there are the roadways of old railroad grades. Fence lines, water tanks, and corruls testify to a longstanding and still active cattle industry. Shrapnel from artillery shells is a reminder of World War II military training. The scattered remains of homesteads tell of a time when dry farming was attempted in this arid land.

Through our Tales of the Mojave Road, many aspects of the early phases of East Mojave history have been documented. Some of the later phases, for example, the cattle industry, mining, homesteading, and others, are equally important and interesting; they too deserve proper documentation so visitors to

7.

that country can be fully aware of its rich history and appreciate and protect the resources there. We have been researching these later historical phases for some time, but it will take many years to process all the data and prepare and publish comprehensive histories.

It is frustrating to have to wait so long to publish something about homesteading, especially when there is a strong demand by lovers of East Mojave history for something more definitive than the few newspaper articles that have appeared.

A few years ago we were fortunate in meeting former East Mojave homesteader Maud Sharp who had written a powerful and poignant personal story about the homesteading experiences of her family. She has granted us permission to publish her reminiscences as a way to enter into this later but fascinating chapter of East Mojave history.

By 1910 the necessary legislation had been passed to enable homestead filings in Lanfair, Pinto, and Round Valleys, and some other well watered areas of the East Mojave. At that time the Searchlight branch of the Santa Fe Railroad was running through Lanfair Valley and hence property ownership in the region looked attractive and potentially profitable. Self-appointed land agents made themselves familiar with available land, location of the survey corners, and other details; then they advertised for homesteaders in Los Angeles area newspapers. They would form a small party of prospective homesteaders and travel by train to the East Mojave to see the land. Of course it was government land and the agent couldn't sell it. But any citizen could file on that land. The agent had knowledge of how to go about it. He charged a fee for his service.

If someone decided to make the break with his existing life and try to make it homesteading on the East Mojave, typically he would select 160 acres, perhaps liquidate his other assets, purchase lumber and tools and provisions, and then hire a railroad car to have his property hauled out to one of the sidings in the East Mojave—generally Ledge (later named Maruba) or Lanfair.

First they would have filed the necessary papers with the General Land Office (forerunner of today's

Bureau of Land Management) and with that they legally commenced their career as homesteaders. They were required to clear a certain amount of the land, plant crops, erect a house and other improvements, and live there most of the time for a specified period. The details varied depending upon the particular laws under which the claim was filed. Once these requirements were satisfied they received a patent and the land was theirs; this all took several years.

This arrangement offered an entirely different way of life for most people. It appealed to those of free and adventuresome spirit; those who felt confined by urban living; or those who wanted to get away from it all and live closer to nature. To top it off, they could go do that and wind up with a piece of potentially valuable land. This arrangement didn't attract ordinary farmers looking for land to farm, it attracted adventurers. Maud and Bert Sharp were adventurers. They felt that at the time.

Homesteads were claimed in the Lanfair Valley area as early as 1910, but the greatest influx was 1912-1915, and also there were many after that. Some pieces were filed on more than once as a homesteader might become discouraged or for some other reason relinquish his claim before proving up.

The original filing by Bert and Maud Sharp on NW¼ Section 7 T13N R17E SBBL&M (a little more than a mile north of Ledge or Maruba) had been filed on by Floyd B. Calvert on January 4, 1913. Calvert had built a home and commenced clearing the land when he decided it was not for him. As mentioned in Maruba, Bert Sharp traded him out of his improvements. Calvert relinquished his claim to the land effective July 3, 1913, and Bert Sharp filed on it that same day. It was not, however, until early the next year that the Sharps moved to Lanfair Valley and commenced homesteading.

It was possible to make a satisfactory living from one of these homesteads. Several people did. Millard F. Elliott, whose homestead was near the Sharps in Lanfair Valley, did it; as did Frank D. Murphy, over by Rock Spring; and Julius D. Alexander and his family in Pinto Valley. But it was a precarious operation at best and the determined homesteader with no supplementary income was destined frequently to

9.

sit down to a meal of beans and jackrabbit.

Rainfall in this part of the world is scanty and unreliable, although there is more rain at this higher elevation (about 4,300 feet at the Sharps' homestead) than there is at most other places on the desert. Crops might be planted and the seeds sprout only to watch them shrivel and dry for want of moisture at the right time. Unfortunately, there was no water supply for irrigation. At other times, a healthy crop might be destroyed overnight by insects or jackrabbits or the multitude of half-wild range cattle that had been there roaming unrestricted on open range long before the homesteaders came.

Many of the homesteaders were forced to find additional sources of income. As will be seen in the story that follows, Bert Sharp filled in this gap laboring for wages on assessment work in the Sagamore Mine, working as "water man" for the Rock Springs Land & Cattle Company, and at one point, he worked in Needles for the Santa Fe Railroad for an extended period during World War I. This pattern was more typical than the few examples where families or individuals did manage to live entirely off the land.

And yet it cannot be concluded that the homesteaders themselves felt they couldn't live there. I once asked Maud Sharp, "At what point did you finally decide you couldn't make a go of it out there; that you couldn't live on that land?" She thought about that for only a moment and with a determined look in her eye and equally determined sound in her voice she replied, "Never! We have always felt we could live on it any time we wanted. Until the day he passed away Bert would mention the possibility of our going back and living there on the homestead."

An entire community developed around the homesteaders of the East Mojave. There were at least two post offices (Lanfair and Maruba), several schools, general stores, and quite an assortment of the trappings of contemporary society. Until 1923 there was regular train service through the valley. The people were not far removed from civilization (which was referred to by them as "inside") because they could catch a train for Goffs and soon be on the main line of the Santa Fe. Fast daily passenger trains would whisk them on into Los Angeles. For social life they had each other. They would meet at the post offices on train days waiting for their mail.

Nearly every Saturday night there was a dance. People from all over the valley attended. Frequently these gatherings were held in school houses, but sometimes in private residences, stores, or in a building designated as the "club house" in Maruba. Usually there was a potluck buffet, sometimes just cake and coffee. These socials could last into the wee hours, and sometimes all night.

The Rock Springs Land & Cattle Company was an important factor in this history. For many years before the homesteaders arrived, this huge ranch was running thousands of head of cattle over as much as a million acres. Mostly it was government land. The company controlled the water either by title or by preemption. The cattlemen were alarmed when homesteaders arrived in increasing numbers, took up large blocks of prime grazing land, and erected fences to keep the cattle out. The focal points of conflict between homesteaders and cattlemen were water and the cattle themselves. The cattle company could (and did in places and at certain times) limit homesteader access to those springs and wells.

With thousands of cattle wandering the open range and with many homesteaders living on beans and jackrabbit, a yearling steer ruining a "nester's" almost ready to harvest crop after breaking through the fence, could be too much to bear. Thus, cattle company beef appeared on the homesteader table; or, at least, the cattle company thought it did.

Bert Sharp worked for the cattle company at one time and they maintained a good relationship. Frequently the Sharps received free beef from the company. Maud Sharp occupies neutral ground with respect to this conflict.

The mining industry in the East Mojave had been much more active in earlier years than it was when the Sharps were there. However, owners of many once active claims were doing annual assessment work in hopes that changes in prices for precious metals would go up and thereby justify reopening the mines. Bert Sharp worked at one of these, the Sagamore, which was one of the oldest mines in the East Mojave.

Maud Sharp provides us with glimpses of many

aspects of life in the East Mojave during those early years. She has written it in a very personal and impressionistic way--in a way that no historian could ever do. She has told us what it was like to be out there in the teens as a young wife and mother trying to make a homestead work. It is the best possible kind of history.

In 1929 when the Sharps returned to live for another year on their homestead, nearly all the earlier homesteaders had left. Many had acquired patent to their land, which was a major objective keeping them there to begin with. It was difficult to make a living under the best of conditions and a series of dry years in the twenties made it nearly impossible, and consequently many others left.

The Alexanders stayed on in Pinto Valley and in fact were probably the last of the old homesteaders to leave when they finally packed up and moved out in 1946. But Bert and Maud Sharp, and many other homesteaders, held on to at least part of their land; they still have it. It is not uncommon at all for one of these old homesteaders or their children to show up in the East Mojave, today, looking over their land. In the back of their minds they are secure in the feeling that they could return to Maruba and make a go of it if they wanted to.

The story that follows is reproduced almost exactly as Maud wrote it over twenty years ago.

Dennis G. Casebier
Chairman
Friends of the Mojave Road

September 23, 1984

12.

CONTENTS

LIST OF ILLUSTRATIONS

LIST OF ILLUSTRATIONS (cont.)

Bert and Maud Sharp in their "going away" clothes on
their wedding day in 1913.
Maud Sharp Collection

16.

Chapter 1

HOMESTEADERS

We were newlyweds and were starting out to make our home in a completely different world from anything we had ever experienced. We had both lived and worked in Los Angeles, the second largest city in California, though at that time a mere village compared to the vast metropolis it has in later years grown to be.

On February 4, 1914, we were athrill with happy anticipation as we boarded the Santa Fe train bound for Ledge, in the Lanfair Valley, California. We, together with several of the other newcomers, had chartered a freight car and had shipped our furniture, household equipment and provisions--all our worldly goods. They would be there when we arrived.

Just six months earlier we, Bert Sharp and Maud E. Morrow, had been married and had spent two happy weeks honeymooning in Avalon on beautiful Catalina Island. The intervening time had been spent in making preparations for this, our big adventure.

Thousands of acres of virgin land had been thrown open by the United States government for homesteading. Any qualified man or woman could file a claim on one quarter section, or 160 acres. About a year later, Congress passed the Enlarged Homestead Act which allowed 320 acres to be taken. Almost everyone had added the extra quarter section to his claim. Later still, the Grazing Act permitted the claiming of a further half section.

To obtain title to a half section, one was required to build a house ten by ten feet or larger, with one door and one window; clear and have under cultivation ten acres the first year, twenty the second, and forty the third; and live on the place seven months each year, for three years.

An acquaintance of Bert's had filed a claim on a quarter section, built a four-room house and a small barn and had cleared ten acres.

They were not happy there, for some reason, and offered to sell his relinquishment. Bert traded his equity in five acres at Terra Bella for the

The weekly train chugs out of Lanfair in the early 1920s on its five mile run to Maruba (below). This comparison shot was made from the identical spot in 1981.
Historical photo John Farmer Collection

19.

relinquishment and improvements, then filed his own claim on the land. We thought it a good trade, for we could move right in without having to put up any buildings, as most of the homesteaders had to do. Later we filed on another quarter section. Ours was half of a small section, giving us 304.59 acres; a portion had been given to the railroad company.

Our train left Los Angeles early in the evening and arrived at Goffs at eight o'clock the next morning where we transferred to the short Searchlight Branch. We had enough time between trains to enjoy a hearty breakfast of oatmeal, ham and eggs, hotcakes and coffee, all for 75 cents each. It was good, too, except for the canned milk which was served with our oatmeal. We had never used canned milk except for cooking, and it would take some time to get used to it. But get used to it we must; there would be no way to get fresh milk.

The Searchlight train was made up of the engine, one combination passenger, baggage and mail car, two or three freight cars and a caboose. Each Monday and Friday a refrigerator car was added for bringing in fresh fruits and vegetables and other perishables.

The valley, about twenty miles long and ten to fifteen wide, is a mile high at our place and somewhat lower (about 3000 feet) at Goffs, in the southern end. Nestled amid lofty mountains, the valley has a spectacular view in every direction. The New York Mountains, with their high needle peaks, lie west; the Piute Range is on the east; and the Hackberry Hills on the south. The Castle Mountains on the north, having the illusive appearance of huge castles, are aptly named.

The trip up the valley to Ledge, our destination, was most interesting to me, since I had not been there before. It was all new and beautiful.

Vegetation was mostly of the desert variety, very green and luxuriant. Fine, fat Hereford cattle grazed tranquilly on the lush grama and other native grasses which were so plentiful.

As far as the eye could see, the mesquite, Spanish bayonets (or daggers), greasewood, many varieties of blooming cactus, the ever-present Joshua tree, and many other native plants and shrubs made a never-to-be-forgotten panorama. The air was so clean and crisp it made us glad to be alive just to be able to breathe it.

At Lanfair, 16 miles north of Goffs, the train stopped to leave the mail and items that were brought in by freight and express. Several children who attended school at Barnwell were taken aboard. Coming back in the afternoon, the train was just in time to pick them up for the return trip home, a round trip of thirty miles daily for the children.

Five miles further brought us to Ledge, our destination. There was no depot at Ledge, but all the trains stopped for fifteen minutes or so--long enough to unload any mail, freight or passengers. There was seldom any passenger boarding the train there.

Most of the settlers in that section of the valley were on hand to meet the train and pick up their mail and any freight or express packages. The mail was brought up from the Post Office in Goffs in a big sack and everyone took what was his. If there was mail for anyone who had not come in that day, it was locked in a large locker and the key kept in a place known to all who received mail there. Transients walking through would not find it so easily.

Everyone greeted us in a friendly fashion. There were Mr. and Mrs. Johnson and their son, Homer; Mr. and Mrs. Ed. Blair and Ed's brother, Jack; John Kousch and his wife, Grace; Mrs. Froman, her brother and her daughter, Mrs. Jacoby; Louis Rochat, Del Block and his mother; George Carruthers and others. We met Mr. Millard F. Elliott, who was to become our best and most beloved friend (and later a partner in a small business venture).

There were also the Barbours: Cecil, his wife and two small children. It was through Mr. Barbour that most of the settlers had come into the valley. He contacted potential homesteaders through advertising and gave them information about the location and general description of the land available, charging a nominal fee. But by going to the land office, anyone could find out for himself where any land open for homesteading was located.

Mr. Barbour's home was located several hundred yards east of the railroad track at Ledge. It was quite a large house, one story, made up of three big

The home of Cecil Barbour in Maruba. Later this belonged to Elanor Jacoby. The "A" frame and water tank mark the site of the well where the Sharps commonly obtained their water. This is the main well at OX Cattle Company Headquarters at Maruba today.

Alice Brownfield and Sam Zimmerman Collection

tents placed end-to-end and framed in with lumber, and had regular windows and doors. There was an extra roof built above and extending out about eight feet in the front for a porch, and the same in back for kitchen and bedrooms. The air space between the two roofs made the house comfortably cool. The Barbours had a good well and sold water to the settlers at twenty-five cents a barrel, as this was the only good well near Ledge.

Mrs. Barbour and I became good friends, though she did not attend any of the dances or picnics. One woman told me she was "stuck-up" and advised me not to have anything to do with her. I never found her that way.

West of the Barbour house and across the railroad track was Mrs. Jacoby's house, with Louis Rochat's on the next section north. The south section line ran about five hundred feet south of the Barbour house, with a roadway between the Barbour and Cordtz claims. With each homesteader taking a section or a half section there were two houses at the most to the square mile. With the distances and the Joshua trees between, there were few houses visible from any one spot.

Laurits Cordtz, whose home was near, asked us to come to their place for lunch. They were a family of five: Laurits, Mrs. Cordtz, Laurits Junior, Minna (about seventeen years old) and a baby. They were typical of the many families who had moved into the valley with high hopes of making a permanent home.

We enjoyed a good lunch and a pleasant, though short, chat with them, after which Mr. Cordtz hauled three barrels of water, our luggage and us to our place, a mile and a half farther north.

Claims had been filed on nearly all the available land in the valley. Many families, fired with the ambition to make homes there in new surroundings were putting up their small houses and moving in. It sounded wonderful--320 acres of good, nearly level land, free!

Chapter 2

WORKING AT SAGAMORE MINE

Here we were, home at last! We were eager to get started on our new life, where we were to have so many new and varied experiences; some were disappointing, of course, but on the whole they were most satisfying.

Our house had a large living room, kitchen, pantry and two bedrooms. After we had cleaned the house and arranged our meager furniture we had a cozy, livable home. There were plenty of good windows with one picture window in the living room, and I had lace curtains for all of them. There was no plumbing. Our bath was a galvanized washtub, our heating system the wood burning kitchen range.

One evening, not long after we arrived, Bert had prepared his bath beside the kitchen stove. Suddenly there was a brilliant flash of lightning followed by a terrific crash of thunder. What appeared to be a ball of fire about the size of a baseball hurtled down along the stove pipe and rolled across the floor to the opposite wall, where it disappeared. It must have been just light and not a concrete substance, because it did not go through the floor or wall. It just vanished in thin air. I couldn't explain it. Looking out the window we saw a Joshua tree in flames about three hundred feet from the house. That was the nearest I have ever been to being struck by lightning. It was an eerie feeling!

Our first project was to get the required ten acres cleared, plowed and ready for planting. Since we had neither horses nor farming implements, Bert cleared land for others in exchange for the plowing and preparing of our land. In the fall, when it was time to plant grain, we seeded our ten acres to rye.

At first, if Bert were late getting home from working for someone else and it was dark, I would not light the lamp but would sit by the window watching for him, imagining I could see someone lurking behind every Joshua tree. Bert whistled almost continuously when he was outside alone. I was always glad when I heard that whistle coming over the ridge about a mile away.

This picturesque road winds through the Joshua tree
forest of Lanfair Valley southwest of Maruba. The
high peaks of the New York Mountains are in the
background.

That first summer the Sagamore Mine, in the New York Mountains, was opened for assessment work. Most of the employees were homesteaders from the valley. Those of us who were married put up tents and did our cooking on hastily built barbecues. It was like a vacation for us.

Mr. and Mrs. Waite were camping near us. He had a six-mule team and wagon which in earlier years he had used to haul ore from the mines around Searchlight, to be shipped out by rail to the mills. He was an able "mule skinner," as he was called, and gave his mules the best of care. Hauling ore and machinery was big business in the early days, and millions of dollars worth of gold, silver, copper and other valuable ores had been taken from those mountains, which were honeycombed with tunnels and shafts. During the years we were at Maruba there was little activity around the mines except for assessment and promotional work.

Sagamore had produced a fabulous amount of gold, it was said, but it had been shut down for years, doing only the annual assessment work that was required to hold the claims.

Mr. Waite was employed hauling some equipment down from the upper part of the canyon to be used at the lower level. The narrow wagon road had been carved out of the mountainside with many sharp curves and steep grades. One day we heard an awful clatter and looked up to see Mr. Waite, mules, and wagon somersaulting down the mountainside, and lumber flying in every direction. The brakes had failed and he had not been able to negotiate the sharp curve. Bert was the first to reach him.

"How are the mules?" was the first thing he asked. He took his knife from his pocket and said, "Cut them loose."

The two big wheelers were down, entangled in the harness. The four others had regained their footing but were badly frightened. Bert cut the harness so they were all free, and the two wheelers were able to get on their feet. Miraculously, there were no bones broken. Except for extensive bruises and scratches they were in good condition after they were calmed down.

The workmen used an old bedspring as a

stretcher to carry Mr. Waite down to the main building, where he was found to have numerous cuts, bruises and abrasions but no serious injuries. There was no doctor there, but Mr. Jacques was skillful in caring for the wounds and in a few days had him back to work.

Frank Jacques was the superintendent at the mine. His wife took care of the kitchen and dining room, cooking the meals for the unmarried men and those whose wives did not move up there. There were about twelve men who boarded with her.

One day Mr. Jacques came down to our tent to talk with me.

"Mrs. Sharp, will you do me a great favor?" he asked. "My wife finds the cooking and dining room work just too much for her. Would you come up and help?"

He said they would furnish both Bert and me our meals for my work, so I agreed to help. Bert was not too happy about it, since he much preferred to eat at home.

Mrs. Jacques was not a talented cook but she always tried to give the men plenty of food. Breakfast was always substantial, with bacon and eggs, hot biscuits and coffee, or hotcakes and bacon--all they could eat. Mr. Jacques always made the hotcakes and they were first-rate. I never tasted better.

Mrs. Waite was the one who taught me to cook red beans, Mexican style, with garlic and chili tepenes, those tiny red hot peppers. She said her mother had told her never to learn to sew; that way someone would have to dress her. But now she was trying to learn. She very proudly showed me a pair of long black cuffs her husband had shown her how to make. They were to be worn over long sleeves to protect them when she was working.

We had to spend at least one night each week on our ranch in order to maintain it as our legal residence. We were calling it "The Ranch" by that time. Mr. Elliott loaned us his horse and light wagon for hauling our camping gear to the mines, but we always walked the four miles down home on Saturday evenings after work and walked back up Sunday afternoons. We enjoyed the walking and were able to

27.

cover the four miles in about an hour.

One Saturday evening we found our door had been forced open and the house ransacked. Our big trunk had been gone through thoroughly. My little pearl-trimmed opera glass was gone. I probably would not have missed it at the time except that the blue velvet bag in which I carried it was left empty. The trunk was filled with seldom used things, so we really did not know just what was missing. A box of pennies and a good supply of canned goods had been taken from the pantry. They were welcome to the food, but Bert was heartbroken when he found that they had taken his little .32 hammerless pistol. It meant so much to him because it had belonged to his father, who had died about six years earlier. They took all his clean socks from his drawer, too, which was an inconvenience, to say the least.

The next week, back at the mine, Bert and two other men were installing a pump. The pump was assembled and they were setting it up with Bert guiding it to the proper place. Before he signaled for them to release it, they dropped it. It caught Bert's forefinger, tearing the end of the finger and the nail completely off.

Mr. Jacques was furious. He said it was pure carelessness on the part of the two who had dropped it. He ordered Bert to bed and had him keep his hand in a basin of warm water to which had been added a little turpentine. He had me add a few drops more of the turpentine at frequent intervals all day, and I kept the water warm.

He kept pacing back and forth across the room, hands behind his back, swearing profanely. He would remember I was there, stop, and say, "Pardon me, Mrs. Sharp. I am just furious about this; it was such inexcusable carelessness." A moment later he would resume his pacing and swearing. Mr. Jacques was a fiery little Frenchman, nervous and excitable, but a very good man. He did his best to see that his workmen were well cared for. He provided safe working conditions as far as he was able.

Bert was able to work again the next day but had to be careful not to tackle a job that would put any stress on the finger, nor to strike it on anything. The finger healed quickly but it took time for the new nail to develop. It grew back to nearly normal but was slightly narrower at the end, and it remained sensitive.

Charley Rosenthal

Chapter 3

UNWELCOME VISITORS

Our house was just a short distance from the railroad track and plainly visible to the many tramps, or transients, passing through. That line was a shortcut and connecting link between the Salt Lake Line at Ivanpah and the Santa Fe main line at Goffs. One day each week the train went to Ivanpah as well as Searchlight—a matter of holding their franchise. The transients who had come to Ivanpah via the Salt Lake freight cars could usually find a way to continue the ride to Goffs. But the other six days they walked the 35-mile track. At Goffs they could go either east or west on the Santa Fe main line.

Our place being so convenient they often stopped and asked for food. A typical approach was this: "Lady, I haven't had anything to eat since yesterday morning and I have been walking ever since." We heard it so often it became a joke, and Bert would frequently come in and repeat it when he wanted coffee or a snack.

Of course, we never refused to give them food. I never let them come in the house when I was alone, but would make sandwiches or give them whatever I had that they could eat outside.

Late one afternoon a man carrying a lunch box came to the door. He said he was looking for work and asked directions to the Sagamore Mine. Bert asked him to come in and we had him eat supper with us. The skies were cloudy and threatening rain, so we let him sleep in our barn on a cot, and I gave him breakfast the next morning. When he left he walked up the road about fifty feet, then as an afterthought, turned and said, "Thanks for the accommodations." They seemed to take any help for granted.

During that first summer, a heavy thunderstorm struck the valley with rain and hail the size of small walnuts. When we returned home the following Saturday we found our roofing paper torn to ribbons and the roof leaking everywhere. Every room showed where the water had poured in. We were a little uneasy when we left the house for a week at a time, and after the roof had been so badly damaged we

30.

This is a view of the Sharp house in 1916, after it
had been moved out of sight of travelers along the
railroad and reduced in size.
Drawing by Charley Rosenthal

decided to tear the house down and rebuild nearer the center of our land, where it would be further from the tracks and partially hidden by some large Joshua trees and shrubbery.

Bert's work at the mine was finished in about six weeks and we moved back home. The settlers all went back to the business of getting their assessment improvement work done on their claims. Since I had earned our board, we had had little expense and had saved most of Bert's earnings. We were able to buy a generous supply of provisions and the seed for planting in the fall.

We started right in on moving the house. Jack Blair, a close neighbor, was a carpenter and agreed to help us with the building, taking as payment enough lumber to build a cook-house for himself, which he could haul around on a wagon to his various jobs. We wanted a smaller house so it was a satisfactory arrangement. When it was finished we had a warm, weather-tight house. The original house had been twice as large, but was poorly constructed and was shaky in a strong wind. We built a large living room, used also as a bedroom, and an eight by twelve kitchen. Soon afterward we added a bedroom.

We were not troubled by tramps either.

Chapter 4

PICNICS & PARTIES

On July Fourth, the Old Settlers Picnic was held at the Lanfair Ranch. Mr. Lanfair ran a small grocery and supply store and the post office. He had a good well about 500 feet deep, one of the few wells in the valley.

People came from miles around: ranchers, cowboys, miners, etc., with their families. Dick Diamond, who had a fabulous reputation as a cook, barbecued the beef. This is approximately the method he used: a few days before the picnic a huge pit was dug and lined with rocks, and a big fire was started in the pit and kept burning until the rocks were sizzling hot. The fire was then removed and the rocks covered with a layer of earth. The three young steers, which had been prepared earlier, were well seasoned, wrapped in canvas, and placed on the earth-covered rocks. More earth, then more heated rocks were added and the whole thing was well covered, sealed with earth, and left to cook slowly to perfection until time to remove it for serving the next day.

The meat was delicious and there was plenty to serve generously the three or four hundred people who attended. There were also beans, salads and all the trimmings, including pies, cakes, and ice cream in abundance. All the women helped to prepare the food. Mrs. Lanfair and the elder Mrs. Farmer supervised everything. I joined several other women in dicing boiled potatoes for salad. Mrs. Farmer was very particular about the potatoes. "When I say diced, I mean diced!" she said. We filled a large-sized tub with carefully diced potatoes. The banquet went off without a hitch.

A pavilion had been erected for dancing, and a piano moved in. Music was furnished by the local folks. There were fiddles, banjos, guitars and harmonicas. There was lively music for the square dances, Virginia Reels, and the Paul Joneses, as well as for the waltzes and two-steps, which were the popular ballroom dances at that time. We loved to dance and were the youngest couple there, and we

A snappy desert roadster parked in front of the
Lanfair Store in the early twenties.
John Farmer Collection

Picture from the 1920s shows railroad tracks in the foreground and Zach Farmer's residence at Lanfair. Indian Hill is in the background.
John Farmer Collection

never lacked for partners. As long as the musicians played, we stayed and danced.

There were many other attractions: horse racing, sack races, potato races, roping and many other contests and games. There was never a dull moment for either young or old. We went to many picnics during our years at Maruba, but this one stands out in my memory as the most successful and the most fun.

There we met just about everyone who lived in the Lanfair Valley, from Goffs to Barnwell, as well as those living in the Pinto Valley, eight miles west of Lanfair. There were outsiders, too, from Needles, Searchlight and the small settlements between.

The Alexanders were one of the first families to move into Pinto Valley. There were several sons and a daughter of fifteen or sixteen. They had grown quite a variety of produce on their place, and later that year they sent invitations to about twenty people to a "Home Products Dinner." We were included. Everything served had been grown on their place except the salt, sugar and seasonings. It was interesting and a huge success. They served chicken, potatoes, cornbread, several different vegetables, fruits of different kinds and milk and butter. She had even made peanut butter from their home-grown peanuts.

Everyone in the valley was asked to come in later for dancing. Mr. Alexander played the piano, and Mrs. Alexander was a wonderful square dance caller. They had built quite a roomy house with a large living room which was filled to capacity with the dancing crowd. We all had a good time and stayed until the wee, small hours.

Water in Pinto Valley was not such a problem. It was closer to the surface than it was in our valley. The Alexanders had a well, and they stayed longer than anyone else, trying to make a home of it. Their place was at a higher elevation than Lanfair, and in addition to the desert vegetation there were juniper, piñon and other trees. There was a nice school building with possibly twenty to twenty-five pupils attending.

Chapter 5

ROCK SPRINGS CATTLE COMPANY

The Rock Springs Land and Cattle Company, with range headquarters at Barnwell, was said to be the second largest cattle growing concern in California; only Miller and Lux, of the San Joaquin Valley, had a more extensive operation.

In earlier years, when the numerous mines in the surrounding mountains were being worked, Barnwell had been a bustling little town of more than a thousand inhabitants. The Santa Fe depot had been a busy spot, handling and shipping ore from mines to mills and also shipping fat cattle to Los Angeles and other markets. The range grasses were so abundant and so nourishing that the cattle were sent direct to market without being put in feed lots for fattening as is done with range stock today. Rainfall has diminished steadily all over southern California through the years so that native grasses and feed have grown less plentiful each year.

The original owner of the Rock Springs Company, Mr. Greening, had died and left the spread to his two sons, Walter and Paul, and to a daughter, Kate, who lived in Los Angeles. The range foreman at Barnwell, Mr. Marvis, was an exceptionally able, well-qualified cattle man. He knew how to run the ranch and was energetic enough to get things done.

In the fall of 1914 Mr. Marvis offered Bert a job on the water detail. Watering places were maintained in numerous locations in the foothills where there were springs or windmills. There were many cuts and fills along the railroad tracks, and during a heavy rain huge ponds--waterholes we called them--would form on the upper sides as drainage from the large watershed of the New York Mountains. Hundreds of head of cattle would water there for weeks at a time, but the cattle company had to be prepared for times when the waterholes were dry. Then there were the troughs in the valley, one three miles southeast of Barnwell and one five miles further down the valley, in the same direction, which were fed by pipeline from the well at Barnwell. These watering places needed to be checked often to be sure that there was

Rock Springs Cattle Company cowboys branding at a
corral in Lanfair Valley during the Homestead period.
Jack Greening Collection

water at all times for the cattle and horses. In that dry climate a few days without water could cause a great deal of damage to the stock.

The Rock Springs brand was "66." Later they purchased the "88" cattle and brand and used that brand on all the new calves. They owned thousands of head of cattle which grazed over a vast area some fifty to one hundred miles in every direction from Barnwell.

That area was, I believe, one of the last open ranges in California, which meant that if a homesteader wanted to grow a crop of any kind he must put up a four-wire barbed wire fence to keep the cattle out. In other areas it was the cattle owner who had the responsibility of keeping his cattle off the cultivated fields. This made a tense situation. The company, who had used the range unopposed for so many years, naturally resented fences going up all over the valley cutting their stock off from so much of the best grazing land. The homesteaders were angry because their fences would sometimes be broken down by the cattle and crops destroyed. The company would sell no beef to the homesteaders and it was rumored that some of the homesteaders were butchering "88" cattle for their own use.

However, we had no trouble with the Cattle Company. They always treated us fairly, and after we worked up there, were very generous with the beef. After butchering, Mr. Marvis would usually bring us down a big roast, or if he were not coming that way, would send it by one of the other riders.

The afternoon we arrived in Barnwell, Mr. Marvis told us to go on in and get our supper, and showed us our room. He was going to be away and would not be eating there that evening.

The kitchen was large with plenty of windows for light and air. The sink, with cold running water, and wood range were along one wall, and a long table was on the other side with chairs for seating about twelve. The "cowpunchers", as they were called, had been coming in and cooking their own meals when they were in Barnwell. There was no one person responsible for keeping the place clean. It showed! Each one would wash his own dishes and cooking utensils. After frying bacon, instead of washing the skillet, they would pour out the drippings and hang the skillet on the wall. On the floor, beneath each skillet, a big cake of grease had accumulated. The whole place was dirty, disorderly and uninviting.

"Bert, let's go up to Whitlows for supper," I said, "I can't cook in here." So we walked over, about two city blocks, and had supper with them.

Mr. Whitlow was the station agent at the Santa Fe depot. They were a year or so younger than we, and we became very good friends.

Next morning I cooked breakfast for Mr. Marvis and ourselves. It was not so bad in the daylight, but with kerosene lamps it had looked so dreary.

"Mr. Marvis," I said, "if you will have someone clean this floor, I will try to keep it clean." There was linoleum on the floor so it was not hard to keep clean once it was scrubbed. Mr. Nicholson, the water man, did the job and I think he never forgave me for that, though he was always friendly and courteous. I gave the place a good cleaning: kitchen, pantry, living room, and our bedroom. The other three bedrooms were not my responsibility.

The punchers rode the range continuously. They would take off from Barnwell, their pack horses loaded with provisions to last as long as they expected to be away--a week or perhaps a month. Their branding irons were always a part of their equipment. They branded all new calves, and kept a close watch over the herds to see that all was well.

They usually carried bacon, potatoes, flour for making biscuits, canned milk and anything else they thought they would need. Always there was "jerky," which is fresh meat (beef was used) cut into thin strips, salted, peppered and hung out to dry for a few days. It could then be kept for weeks, eaten "as is" or cooked in various ways.

As when we were at the mine, we returned to the ranch to spend Saturday nights. Sometimes we would take the train down on Friday afternoon. It did not run on Saturday or Sunday, so we walked the eight miles back Sunday afternoon. That gave us a good workout. We checked our speed by the mile posts along the track and covered a mile in fifteen minutes regularly.

Usually we took the buckboard and team or rode

Maud Sharp on "Shrimp" at Rock Springs
Land & Cattle Company Headquarters in Barnwell.
Maud Sharp Collection

saddle horses. Mr. Marvis always kept a string of horses in the corral for his personal use and these were the ones he gave us to ride. I had done no riding since leaving Tennessee, when I was twelve years old, and knew nothing about riding western style. It is quite different from riding eastern style!

The first time we rode, Mike, one of the punchers who had come in off the range that day, was told to saddle a good gentle horse for me. The road ran past an old deserted saloon building. I kept pulling on the left rein but old Eagle just went straight on and almost landed in the building. Finally, Bert said, "Don't pull the reins; just lay them across his neck to tell him which way to go." From then on I had no trouble, but when we rode back to Barnwell the next day we exchanged horses. The other was a little bay saddle horse that was a joy to ride, and we grew to love him. His name was Shrimp. It was a truly descriptive name. Eagle was used mostly as a pack horse, and we never rode him again.

We had bought a little old mare called Lady and a light spring wagon for hauling water and supplies. While we were working away from home she was on the range with other horses, but would stay near the house. On our way back to Barnwell we drove her over to the Three Mile trough so she would always have fresh water. As soon as we headed in that direction Shrimp seemed to know what we were trying to do. Every time Lady would start to leave the trail he would be off to turn her back before we even noticed. We had her there in a short time and rode on into Barnwell by the back way. From that time on we rode Shrimp and Beanbelly (Beans for short) most of the time. Sometimes we would take Sam. He had a mean eye, so they said, and could be hard to manage. Bert usually rode him, but I did take him a few times. He never misbehaved with me. Mr. Marvis was a little afraid to have me ride him. He was afraid I might get hurt.

We always started out walking the horses. After we were on the road, if Beans got a nose ahead of Shrimp, Shrimp would pull out ahead. Each one wanted to lead and if we gave them their heads, they would soon be having a race. It was such fun! But

Dick and Matilda Diamond at their home in Barnwell.
John Farmer Collection

we never let them run very much. Mr. Marvis was very particular about the way they were handled. He never wanted them to get hot and lathered with sweat. He was just as careful about the cattle and spent many hours riding around inspecting the herds. If he found any that looked weak or under par, he would bring them in and feed them, or have hay hauled out to them on the range.

At the time we were in Barnwell there was not much left of the town. There were the Cattle Company buildings--the main house, two small one-room bunkhouses, the barn, corral and slaughterhouse. Across the railroad to the south were the houses of the railroad workers. The station and loading platform were in the angle formed where the branch of the railroad went off to the east. North of the Cattle Company house was a large two story house, and across the railroad to the west was the old saloon as well as several small houses.

Besides the Whitlows, other inhabitants were Mr. Morse, the postmaster; Mr. Spear, a prospector; the railroad section foreman and his crew; and the Rock Springs employees.

And there was Dick Diamond, too, a black man who was a legendary figure throughout the mining country. He was called "One-Eyed Dick." One eye had been badly damaged in a fight years before. He would never say whether he could see through that eye, but I'm quite sure his sight was gone. He and his wife, Matilda, lived quietly in a little cottage that was always as neat as a pin.

The Greening boys came out occasionally to spend a few days. When I met Walter the first time he was out, the resemblance to a Miss Greening, who had been my cooking teacher at school about eight years earlier, was so striking that I asked him about a sister.

"Yes," he said, "My sister did teach cooking at that time." Her name was Kate. It is amazing the people we meet in such unexpected places!

Walter was always very active while at the ranch. He was up at the crack of dawn out riding the range. He took a great interest in every phase of the business. Paul was more quiet and was content to spend his time around the house during his

This roundup scene at White Rock Tank on the Kessler Springs Ranch (a descendant of the Rock Springs Company) was taken in 1984 -- but it would have looked the same in Maud Sharp's time. Gary Overson is the cowboy swinging the lasso.

Water tank showing "88" brand at
White Rock Spring on Cima Dome.

infrequent visits.

We will never forget the first time they butchered after we arrived! Mr. Marvis always selected a four-year-old cow; he said that made the best beef. I cooked a big platter of round steak. How we did go for it! It really was tender and good down to the very last small cuts. But I suspect that one reason we enjoyed it so much was that fresh meat was difficult for us to get and to keep without refrigeration. Other than bacon and ham, our meat was mostly of the canned variety.

We did have quail and cottontail as often as we liked. They were numerous and Bert could go out any time and bring home enough for a meal. Doves were also plentiful but he seldom shot those. We never felt that they should be classed as game birds.

I prepared the meals for Mr. Marvis and any guests who might come in, such as Walter and Paul Greening, or an occasional cowboy who happened to ride in for a day. But when several of the crew came in at once, they stayed in the bunkhouse. They had a cookhouse where they could prepare their own meals.

The diet was rather limited as far as variety was concerned. We always had a pot of red beans on the stove. There was beef most of the time, plenty of bacon, potatoes, canned milk and tomatoes. Mr. Marvis was good about bringing fresh fruits and vegetables from Ivanpah when he could get them, but they were not always available. I baked bread, a few pies and cakes. All in all we had plenty.

Bert thoroughly enjoyed working with horses and the cowboys. Once he was sent with the crew over to Searchlight to be gone overnight. They were checking on the cattle and the watering places in that area. They had a great time around the campfire that night. Several burros, probably belonging to prospectors, wandered into camp. Bert tried getting on one but without bridle or saddle he couldn't make it. Mike proceeded to build a very creditable bridle from a piece of rope. Bert was able to get on the burro, but even with the bridle he was tossed off every time and had several sore spots where he hit the ground. But he always went back for more. He, being a tenderfoot, was subject to a great deal of ribbing. He took it all with good grace and as a result made good friends of the boys.

After they had gone I was sitting at the table looking through the Sears' catalogue. Mr. Marvis had said it would be all right for me to order material to make curtains for the living room windows so I was trying to find something suitable. He was sitting over by the stove. It was a cold morning. I asked him to come over and look at what I was considering.

"Anything you choose will be all right," he said.

He came over and sat on the table and as I started to show him the book he reached out suddenly and put his right arm around my head and drew me over to him. My reaction was swift and to the point. I slapped him as hard as I could.

"Ouch!" he exclaimed. "That hurt."

"I meant it to hurt," I said.

He got off the table and walked back to his chair. I went into my room, picked up a few things I would need for overnight, came back through the kitchen, and told him that I would spend the rest of the day and the night with the Whitlows.

"You don't have to go away. I will not bother you any more." he said.

"Why did you do that?" I asked.

"Because I like you," he answered.

"Well, I don't like that kind of business."

"I see you don't. You can stay here as long as you like. I will never bother you again."

I was sure he meant it, but I went on to the Whitlows anyway.

Next day he sent a message to Bert, by the train conductor, to come back on the afternoon train. I was surprised when I saw he had returned.

When I told him what had happened, he said, "I will tell Mr. Marvis we are through and are leaving." But I told him that would not be necessary; I was quite sure there would not be any more trouble. He never mentioned the matter to Mr. Marvis. We just ignored the whole thing. Mr. Marvis became our good friend, and remained so for all the years we were at Barnwell.

I was extremely naive. I never dreamed that he would ever think of such a thing. He was at least twenty years older than I and I had looked on him as an employer, or more nearly as a father or brother, so I was shocked.

Afterwards, In fairness, I had to admit to myself, at least, that he might have taken it as an invitation when I asked him to come over and look at the catalogue. But in all truth, that was the farthest thing from my mind. I guess I was stupid as well as naive!

WALTER GREENING
GENERAL MANAGER

PHONE DOWNEY A284

Rock Springs Land and Cattle Company
(INCORPORATED)

BRAND
88

BRAND
53

NORWALK, CALIF.

June 4th, 1926.,

Chapter 6

OUR FIRST CHILD

We were at Barnwell three months, until late January, 1915, when we moved back to the ranch. One day Mr. Marvis let Mrs. Whitlow and me take two of his saddle horses and go riding in the hills. The horses were always ready to run and we allowed them to do so for a short distance. Suddenly I had a sharp pain in my side and had to slow down. The pain persisted until after we reached home. About that time I discovered that I was pregnant. That was the reason for the pain in my side, when we were out riding.

The idea of having a baby way out there, with the nearest doctor fifty miles away in Needles, and he a Santa Fe doctor, did not appeal to us. Our only means of transportation was our little one-horse outfit. That was before the "Two Cars in Every Garage" era.

Our required improvements were finished and we had lived on the ranch the necessary amount of time so we were allowed to be away one year. We made plans to go back to Los Angeles and stay until after the baby was born. Mother Sharp lived in her six-room house on Glendale Boulevard and there was always room there for us. While with her we paid all the grocery bills, utilities, and usual expenses of running a house, but having no rent to pay was a big help.

Those next few weeks should have been happy ones for us, as we began to prepare for our new son. It did not work out quite that way. I was more unhappy then than at any other time in my whole life. Some dear friends of the family thought it would be just criminal to take an infant out to that "wilderness," as our place seemed to them to be. They couldn't understand that we loved every minute of it. The freedom and peace and the opportunity to live our own lives were very precious to us.

Then Mother Sharp began to worry about it too. They wanted to take me to a doctor who would get rid of the baby for me. I was horrified! Never for one moment did I consider doing away with my baby, but all the talk did sow a seed of apprehension in my mind. Just suppose he were sick, and we were not able to get him to a doctor in time. What would we do? I know nothing about the care of a baby. Although we were a large family, I was one of the younger ones and did not have the care of the little ones as my older sisters had. I knew that babies do become ill and sometimes die, even when a doctor is doing all he can to save them. So I worried about what might be in store for us.

Our philosophy has always been, "Every problem has a solution. With the help of God and by our own efforts we could find that solution."

Bert was calm about it all and said, "Don't worry; everything will be all right."

My eldest sister, Mai, was my "Rock of Gibraltar," a firm support in my time of weakness. A talk with her gave me the courage and serenity I needed and I soon forgot my anxiety about the future.

Her husband, John Sheets, was a real friend also. Mai promised to take care of me when the baby came, and John made us feel it would be a pleasure to have us with them. They had two darling children--Thelma, about ten years old and Johnny, four. When the baby came and ever after he was such a joy to us that we have felt repaid many times over for any anxiety we may have felt.

Unemployment was widespread at that time. Bert had had over five years' experience in the Crane Company plumbing supply house in Los Angeles, but could find nothing in that line. After looking for work a couple of weeks without success he found a job of sorts, passing out sample packages of corn flakes. That was quite a comedown, but he pocketed his pride and went at it. A truck load of sample packages was driven into a designated neighborhood with six men aboard. Each man took a big bag of the packages and delivered them from house to house, six days per week. They were paid the munificent sum of $1.50 a day. After six weeks Bert was called to the plumbing supply house and had steady work until we were ready to return to Ledge.

In the meantime I met a girl who worked in the ladies' tailoring shop where I had been employed until my marriage. She said Mr. Friedman needed a skirt maker, which was my line of work. When she told him I was in town, he sent word asking if I would come to work for him. I was glad to do so and worked as long as I could, until June first. I was becoming heavy and awkward by then, although I was in perfect health.

The rest of the summer passed uneventfully. True to her promise, Mai had us move in with her and her family when it was nearly time for the baby. On September 28, early in the evening, we called Dr. Sherer.

Mai had invited Mother Sharp over for dinner that evening, not knowing that was the day we were waiting for, so unintentionally, she was there for the party.

At 11:50 p.m. our son arrived, just ten minutes ahead of the deadline on his father's birthday. We were all elated that their birthdays were on the same day and could be celebrated together. We have been fortunate enough to have them together on their birthdays every year since, except for the six years Jim served in the Navy during World War II, and two years after the war was over.

We stayed with Mai and John until the baby was four weeks old. We named him James Clifton, after his Grandfather Sharp whom I had never met. He had died several years before I knew Bert.

We moved back to Mother Sharp's where we remained until Jimmy was four months old. Then, on February 1, 1916, we once more packed our belongings and made the trip back to Ledge. We shipped a young heifer out there, and when she came fresh we had plenty of milk, butter and cream.

Jimmy Sharp seated at the base of a Joshua tree in front of the Maruba Post Office in 1916.
Maud Sharp Collection

Chapter 7

BACK TO SAGAMORE MINE

A number of changes greeted us on our return to Ledge. A post office had been established with M. F. Elliott as postmaster. Since there was a Ledge, California, with a post office in another part of the state, we had to select a new name for ours. There was a man in the area whose father had served as captain on a ship named *Maruba* and he suggested that name. It was chosen from a list of names submitted, and from that time on it was Maruba instead of Ledge.

Cecil Barbour had sold his place to Mrs. Jacoby, whose land adjoined his on the west. She now owned the well and sold water to the settlers at the reduced price of 15 cents a barrel. She had moved into the Barbour house. The one she had vacated was built with a very large living room, small kitchen and bedroom. It made an ideal place for people to gather for dances, picnics and other purposes. It was called the Club House. We had many good times there. Across the road from the Club House a small building had been erected to house the post office.

We found our place as we had left it. We were wise in moving over where it was not so easily seen from the tracks.

We need never have worried about taking Jimmy out there. He was a healthy, happy baby and grew into a strong, sturdy boy. He and I spent many happy hours looking for wild flowers and interesting plants and trying to classify as many birds by name as we could. He was eager to learn about everything he saw.

In late Spring, Sagamore was again opened, under new management. Mr. Doake was the new manager with Mr. Hinckley as the superintendent. Bert, along with other homesteaders, went up again to work, and again we moved up there. This time we were quite comfortably situated. We had fashioned a tent 12' by 16' from a larger tent that had been on our place when we moved out there. It had been very hard to handle, as large as it was, so we cut it down and sewed the ends in by hand, backstitching every seam twice. We made the walls six feet high. We had two windows with mosquito netting sewed in and canvas curtains outside which we could roll down to close them, and a door with netting, also.

We chose a spot beside a large piñon tree for our tent, several hundred yards below the mine proper. When Mrs. Doake found out we had a baby, she insisted that her husband have the men bring lumber, build a frame for our tent, and put in a floor. There was room for our bed, table, chairs and cookstove, and plenty of wood nearby for fuel.

Bert built a small playpen and hung it, as a swing, from a large branch of the piñon tree just outside the door. I padded it well and lined it. Jimmy would play happily there for hours at a time, safe from snakes and other crawling things on the ground. There were many things to attract his attention: people moving about, horses near by, many birds flying around the trees, and squirrels, lizards and chipmunks on the ground.

We took our cow along and kept her staked out in the grass not far away so we had plenty of milk. I sold three quarts a day to Mrs. Doake, who had three little girls. We also had our few hens. They supplied us with fresh eggs. They stayed around the mangers where the horses and mules were fed and picked up most of the grain they needed. Some hid nests out in the brush and hatched their chicks.

There was no refrigeration, of course, but we made a desert cooler which kept food surprisingly well. It was a box frame, screened and covered with burlap, with shelves and hinged door. We kept an olla, or large jar, full of water on top, from which strips of absorbent cloth, such as cotton flannel, hung down over the burlap keeping it wet. There was always enough breeze to keep it cool. Cream kept there was cool enough for whipping. Because of the perfect circulation through and around it, there was never any odor.

No matter how hot the day, evenings in that climate are cool and relaxing. After supper some of the workmen, some with their wives, would stroll down and settle themselves comfortably around our campfire and spend the evening singing, telling tall tales or just talking. There was usually some light refreshment: a bit of cake or pie, and coffee or perhaps a glass of milk. The air was so clear the stars seemed very close. On moonlight nights it was light enough for traveling anywhere.

Since work started at eight o'clock next morning the parties broke up early. They had to get back to their tents for a good night's sleep.

Mr. Hinckley, the superintendent, took his meals in the camp dining room with the men. There was plenty of hearty food but little in the line of desserts. He was very fond of milk and often dropped in for a glass or two. I was the only one up there with a regular kitchen stove and oven. I baked our bread, cakes and pies, so he usually had something fresh from the oven with his milk. One day when he came I had just finished baking a big chocolate cake. I set a pitcher of milk and my fresh cake on the table and invited him to help himself. He ate nearly half the cake, and I don't know how much milk he drank, but he said, "For once I have had all the milk I could drink." It was a pleasure to us to watch him enjoy it.

During his stay at Sagamore, Mr. Hinckley conducted Sunday services in the Club House at Maruba. Every one came, regardless of denomination, and enjoyed his interesting and inspiring talks, the singing of old, familiar hymns and the general atmosphere of friendliness. After services, tables were set up and loaded with the picnic foods contributed by all of us. A great favorite was Mrs. Bell's whipped cream cake, a big four layer cake with whipped cream filling and frosting. There was never any of that left.

Those Sunday meetings gave each of us a lift and were sadly missed after Mr. Hinckley left the valley.

One day a rider from the Cattle Company came by and brought us a huge roast from a freshly butchered beef. There was so much of it! I cooked as much as we would be able to eat, and then made 'jerky' of the rest. Later I told Mr. Marvis what I had done.

He said, "I thought you would have sense enough to take care of it." The piece that had been intended for us was smaller but had been taken to Mrs. Guirado's family at Lanfair by mistake. There

Anson Murphy used a tractor to clear and cultivate
Pinto Valley land in the late teens.
Anson Murphy Collection

were many children in the Guirado family, and they were to have had the larger piece of beef.

Everything went along smoothly at the mine until the assessment work was done. Bert did not work in the mine itself but did plumbing and remodeling and repair work on the buildings. His work was finished earlier than that of some of the others who had teams and would be working a few weeks longer.

We figured our tent was getting old, and when Mrs. Brown wanted to buy it, we sold it to her for $7.50. The day after we left she sold it to Ed Blair for $25.00. What easy marks we were!

I wonder now how we ever got our land cleared and planted when we were away so much, earning our bread and butter. It was no small job grubbing out the tough roots of the greasewood, cat's claw, and other brush. The Joshua trees were not so difficult nor the Spanish daggers. Somehow we did get it done. I say "we;" I did little except to help burn the brush, as much of it as possible, and to be there lending my moral support. We usually had Jimmy out with us.

There were dances in the Club House, which were well attended, and we had such good times. Jimmy would go to sleep soon after we arrived, so we had the evening free for dancing. There were cots in the bedroom where the sleeping children could be made comfortable. Bert liked to sit on the sidelines and talk, but I seldom missed a dance. There were more men than women, so we were kept busy. The lively square dance, Virginia reel, and the Paul Jones soon had every one feeling right at home and having a wonderful time. There were always refreshments, usually cake, cookies, and coffee.

Chapter 8

RETURN TO BARNWELL

Mr. Marvis came in one day and asked Bert if he would come up to Barnwell for a few weeks and take the place of Mr. Nicholson, the water man, who was going on a vacation. He was going to England to bring his wife back with him. Bert agreed.

Jimmy was seven months old. Mr. Marvis took quite a fancy to him. He would carry him around, play with him, and take care of him for hours at a time.

We were there a short time when a family rode in from Arizona. There were Mr. Jim Craig; his son Tommy, seventeen years old; a younger son, a daughter and her husband, with several of their young children. Mr. Craig had been hired as a cowhand; the others were looking for work. Mr. Marvis put Tommy and the son-in-law on the payroll.

After they were there a few days, Bert had a talk with Mr. Marvis, telling him it was too much work for me and that we had better leave. I hadn't agreed to cook for so many people. After all, Bert's salary was only $40.00 a month and my work was gratis.

"No," Mr. Marvis said. "You stay here. I'll take care of it."

There were a number of vacant, deserted houses in Barnwell. He had a large two-story one cleaned up and moved in enough furniture so that the Craigs could camp there. They were friendly and cooperative and the daughter helped with the work while they were there. She showed me how to make a jerky gravy that was really good. She roasted the jerky in the oven until it was crisp, then pounded it with a hammer on a flat piece of iron into very small pieces, some of it almost powder. She heated a little shortening in a skillet, stirred in and browned some flour, added the jerky and enough milk to make a gravy of the desired consistency, stirring until it was thoroughly blended and cooked. With hot biscuits or mashed potatoes, it was a dish fit for a king. She also taught me how the Mexican women prepare the dry red chilis by roasting them in the oven until the skins could be easily removed and discarded. The remainder was then crushed to use for seasoning.

As usual, when Mike came in for dinner one day, I had a pot of beans on the stove. I had added three or four of the little hot chili tepenes, which made it hot enough for us. Mike dished out a big plate of beans and crushed a dozen or more extra chili tepenes over them. I thought surely his mouth would have to be lined with asbestos to get away with that! But he enjoyed it.

Bert worked until the latter part of August. We needed to get back to the ranch and finish our planting. He had the water department under control, and Mr. Nicholson was due back any day. While we were packing our things getting ready to go, Mr. Marvis had Jimmy in his high chair and was feeding him grapes. He very carefully removed the seeds and skins. Jimmy was having a grand time. I had not fed him much except eggs, cereal, and toast. Of course, he had plenty of milk. I thought the grapes would not hurt him.

Next day he was a really sick baby. I was alarmed, but gave him some castor oil prepared especially for babies. He took very little food all day. The second day he was better, but it was several days before he was back to normal. I know now that he was more seriously ill than I realized at the time. Now I would be panic-stricken were I in that situation. That was the only time he was ill while we were on the ranch.

A week later Mr. Marvis rode down and brought us a fresh beef roast. We were seldom without fresh meat from that time on as long as he was there.

He told us they were having trouble with Pinto Valley people butchering their cattle. He had heard that they would all get together on the deal. Some would stand watch on the surrounding hills, to give the alarm should riders be seen near, while others did the butchering. Then the meat would be divided among them.

Mr. Marvis really did not mind too much if they used the meat for themselves, but some were peddling it regularly in the small settlements along the highway. That was adding insult to injury!

One day two men were caught red-handed. They

were arrested and spent some time in jail in San Bernardino. Things were better for a time.

Someone had given Mr. Marvis a little dog called Teddy. He was supposed to be a collie, but grow to be only about half as large as a normal collie. He followed Bert around most all the time. Bert has always been a great lover of dogs and they return his affections. When we used the team and buckboard to move back home, Teddy followed us.

Mr. Marvis, as usual, was riding, and when he started home Bert said, "Mr. Marvis, here is your dog. You had better take him with you!"

"Let him pick his choice," he replied.

Teddy chose to stay with us. We had him about two years. Then, he followed someone over to Pinto Valley and never came back.

We had heard that a dog would never tackle a coyote. That did not prove true with any of our dogs, not even little Teddy.

One day Jimmy was sitting out in the yard playing in the sand. I was ironing just inside the open door and looked out to see a coyote walking across the yard just a few feet from where Jimmy was playing. At first glance I thought it was a neighbor's dog, but with a second look I realized it was a coyote. Teddy was there and started after it, nipping at its heels. When it turned on him, he would jump back until it started away again, then lunge at its heels. He kept it slowed down enough that Bert had time to get out there with the gun and was able to shoot it just as it reached the fence.

Some years later, we were keeping a big Lewellyn setter for a friend in Los Angeles who had wanted the dog to have a place where he could run and have enough exercise to keep trim and alert.

Early one morning I saw a coyote eating a watermelon in our melon patch. The setter saw him about the same time and started for him. The last I saw of Mr. Coyote he was going over the top of a low hill, the dog close behind, tail waving briskly as it disappeared from sight. We didn't know whether the dog caught up with him, but when he came home there was no sign of battle.

In May, 1962, Bert and I returned home from Arizona by way of Maruba, after visiting my sister

Bee. We stopped there at the headquarters of the OX Cattle Company, successors to the Rock Springs Cattle Company. We had a long and interesting talk with the woman who was in charge of cooking for the ranch hands. She told us of many things that had happened since we left, and about many of the people we had known. She said she had attended the party celebrating Jim Craig's ninety-sixth birthday a few months before, and that he had died shortly afterward.

Charley Rosenthal

Chapter 9

COMPANY

Late in November, 1916, my parents, my sister Belle, her husband Barb Moser and their two boys, Tourist and Dale, came by our place on their way to Los Angeles. They had proven up on their homesteads in San Pedro Valley in Arizona and had sold their land. A sister-in-law, Myrtle, was with them and also my younger brother, Fred.

An hour or so before they arrived, Jimmy had finished his breakfast and was sitting in his high chair playing with a toy. When I stepped out of the room for a moment, he started rocking back and forth. He could propel himself all around the room that way. Just as I returned, the chair went over and he fell on his face, striking his mouth on a kitchen cabinet. His teeth cut his lip quite badly. His mouth was swollen and very sore and for the rest of the day he cried when he tried to eat or drink milk. As a result, when the folks came he would have nothing to do with them. My Dad said he was just like a little wild jackrabbit, scared of everything. He teased us about it for years. Really, Jimmy would make friends with anyone when he was himself, but he hurt so much he wasn't interested.

It was not a propitious time for a crowd to come. Bert had built a water tank of galvanized sheet iron that would hold four barrels. It would fit on our wagon and be more convenient for hauling water. It took longer to make than he had expected and he had put off getting water until it was finished. So we were completely out of water when the folks came, with the supper and breakfast dishes yet to be washed. Bert was at the well filling the tank when they passed. He arrived home with the water a few minutes after they came. The sheet metal was not heavy enough and buckled at the seams. Some of the water was lost, but there was plenty to last through the two days they were there. Later Bert repaired and reinforced the tank and it proved very useful.

What with the dirty dishes and the cross baby, I was somewhat upset. But, "all's well that ends well," and we had a wonderful time. Belle was so competent;

she brought order out of the chaos in short order. Barb was also a big help. He dressed one of our turkeys and we had all the trimmings, so food was not a problem.

The big question was where they would sleep. With our two rooms and our one bed it was a knotty problem, but it worked out very well and we had a lot of fun.

Bert brought in some bales of alfalfa hay and spread it along the length of our living room and covered it with a canvas tarpaulin. We then opened up two pairs of double blankets for warmth.

Mother, the baby and I slept on the bed; the other eight lined up side by side on the hay bed and said they slept well. They stayed for two nights.

Mother liked our place. She said the soil looked like it would grow anything, but Dad said he would not live there for the whole valley. He wanted to be nearer a city, where there was a little excitement.

Bert had no work in sight and it was nearing the time for us to prove up on our claim, which would require a little money. Mother, Dad and Belle talked it over with Bert and persuaded him to let them take Jimmy and me home with them so he would be free to go out and find work.

The evening before we left, Dad and Barb spent hours patching inner tubes punctured during the two days' travel from their places in Arizona. Each of them had bought a new 1916 Model T Ford touring car. Tires in those days were expensive and gave little service.

We left the ranch early next morning. I nearly reneged and stayed there, Bert looked so forlorn at seeing us go. But we each put up a brave front when we said goodbye.

It was a three hundred mile journey--too long to be made in one day over those roads. There were no paved nor graded roads, but plenty of rocks, sand, and chuck holes! At Barstow, the half way point, Dad had to buy a new tire. We spent the night there and reached Dad's home next afternoon.

In spite of the tire trouble we had a good time on the trip. It was good to be with my people again. I often think how awful it would be not to have a family. Mine has meant so much to me, through the years: my four brothers, four sisters, and the best parents in the whole world.

Jimmy and I were having a grand time. There were so many to make a fuss over him and over me, too. We were living it up. But it did not last long. I received a letter from Bert saying, "Come on back home. Life isn't worth living like this. I'm sure we can manage and still be together."

We missed him, too, in spite of all the folks were doing to give us a good time. I think Jimmy was showing that he missed him. When we would be walking on the street, he would want to go to every man we met. So I packed up our clothes and went back. It was a happy reunion when Bert met us at the train.

Chapter 10

HOLDING THE FORT ALONE

Whenever there was a cloudburst in the mountains, the dry washes would be filled from bank to bank with a rushing torrent of water, and sections of the railroad tracks would often be washed out. Shortly after we returned home, several long stretches were washed out between Goffs and Maruba. This time, it was six weeks before the repair work was done and trains running again. My youngest brother, Tom, had come up to see us and was there during that time. We had sent in a large order for groceries just before the washout, but with no train, there were no groceries.

Before the trains began running again our groceries were running low. I had used the last of the flour. There was a problem! How was I to make bread? We tried grinding wheat in a small coffee mill. I made it up as I would make corn bread. It was delicious. I also used milo maize in the same way. It was good, too. I tried making bran bread, but we did not care for that. We had the wheat, milo and bran in hundred-pound sacks, so we had plenty of that. We would spread the grain on the table and remove any weed seeds and chaff before grinding. It was quite a task and one in which we all took a hand. We still had canned goods. We tried to keep enough of the staples to carry us through any emergency. We were still milking the cow so there was milk. Bert and my brother Tom were both appreciative of my efforts to create something tasty of what we had on hand.

To some, I suppose, a thing like that would be a trial and a hardship. To us it was just another challenge to our ingenuity, another problem to be solved. Typical of our way of life, we never thought of trying to borrow from our neighbors. If we didn't have what we wanted, we could always find something else that we could use instead.

Mr. and Mrs. Nay and their small children came over to spend the day during the time of the washout. As they had not let us know beforehand that they were coming, she brought food. With what additions I could make, we had a good dinner. They had been accustomed to drinking canned milk and didn't like the fresh. Luckily, I had some cans of milk, too.

After Tom had been with us for about a week, he said to me, "This is the first time since I was grown that I have been without a headache. I just thought that was part of growing up." He had suffered greatly with sinus trouble. The high altitude and clean air relieved it completely. It never troubled him so much again. But it did come back in milder form after he returned to Los Angeles.

Tom, who was seventeen, loved children. He thought Jimmy was just about right. When Bert would be out working around the shop or barn, Jimmy would follow him everywhere. It amused Tom when Bert wanted to come to the house that Bert would pick Jimmy up, toss him across his hip like a sack of meal, and carry him in. Jimmy loved it.

"Oh boy! Just wait until I have four or five of these of my own. The world is mine!"

"When I come home they will all run to meet me and I'll have something in every pocket for them, and they will go through my pockets until they find everything."

It was sad that his dream never came true. His wife lost their first after about five months of pregnancy and the doctor told her that she could never have another. Later, they adopted an infant boy and a girl a few days old. They were about a year apart in age. As they grew up I heard him say many times, "I know I could never love one of my own any more than I love these."

It happened that Mrs. Jacoby's well broke down frequently during that winter, due partly to the cold. Then, too, the pump had been used for several years and was beginning to wear out. Bert was called in each time to repair it. It seemed to quit just often enough for Bert to earn money to keep us in groceries that winter.

In the summer, July 16, 1917, he went to Needles to work in the tin shop at the Santa Fe roundhouse.

Jim Noyes, a friend, was in charge of the shop and told Bert there was an opening and that he could have the job. Mr. Noyes had filed a homestead claim in the valley. Later he married a widow, Mrs. Whitney, who was proving up on her own homestead so he dropped his.

We still had two months to live on our place in order to prove up. I agreed to stay there with Jimmy and let Bert go to Needles to work. He could come home Sundays when he did not have to work, but the work week was ten hours a day, six days a week, with every other Sunday on the job. He was also a member of the company fire department and had to answer every alarm, day or night. So he did not come home very often.

The time passed pleasantly enough. Jimmy was nearly two years old and was lots of company. I had never minded being alone too much. There was always something interesting to do or to read. I never tired of walking over the countryside with Jimmy just to see what interesting things we might find.

Since the mines in Searchlight and the surrounding mountains were no longer operating, there was little business for the railroad, either freight or passenger. The trains no longer came through every day but only on Fridays and Mondays. The depot at Barnwell had been closed and Clint Whitlow, the agent, had been transferred to Needles and was now living there with his family. They had a boy, Bobby, two months younger than Jimmy.

On train days Jimmy and I would walk down to Maruba, about a mile and three quarters each way. He usually tired before we reached home, but after a short rest, he would always be able to make it.

One day, when we were in Maruba, Mr. Tim Nay said his wife wanted him to bring Jimmy and me up to their place for dinner. We spent the day with them and then he drove us back home. He had a Pathfinder automobile, one of the few cars in the valley. Mrs. Nay had not been well and seemed happy to have us. Jimmy had fun playing with the children and it was a pleasant outing for me. They were one of the few families who had a regular income. He was watchman at the Gold Chief Mine.

Nearly all the homesteaders had to haul water. If they got it at the well in Maruba, then they paid 15 cents a barrel. They could drive the few extra miles up to the mine and get all they wanted for nothing.

Everyone had to solve the water problem. These Pinto Valley boys are headed to Rock Springs to obtain the family water supply.
Anson Murphy Collection

69.

Mr. Nay would pump it for them, without charge. With team and wagon they could haul two to four barrels at a time so many of them took advantage of the opportunity. It was such a lovely spot in the mountains and a pleasant drive up there that it made a nice outing for the families, and they usually went along.

The Nays were friendly and hospitable people, and always invited families to have lunch with them. It became a dreadful nuisance after a while. With several guests for lunch every day, Mrs. Nay had no time to do her own work. Also, it was expensive. She found a clever way of putting an end to it. She posted a sign over the door, "MEALS, 35¢."

I never had a light in the house at night when Bert was away. We would have our supper before dark and then I would sit in the twilight singing to Jimmy or telling stories until he would fall asleep. Then I would turn in. We would be ready to get up early in the morning.

Mrs. Whitlow and Bobby came up from Needles one Friday and stayed until Monday with Jimmy and me. Her husband was working a relief shift at Searchlight.

While Mrs. Whitlow was with me, the two of us were brave enough to light the lamps. On Sunday evening a big storm came up with sharp lightning and thunder and heavy rainfall. Our boys were asleep and we were enjoying a cozy little chat, trying to get caught up on our talking, when suddenly we heard horses galloping down the road straight toward our house. It sounded like there were six or eight of them. We thought it must be a bunch of drunken riders to be out on a night like that and we were scared. We barricaded the doors with dressers, tables, and the heaviest furniture we had. Bert always wanted me to keep the revolver handy just in case, so we got that and a shotgun out, ready for business, blew out the lights and waited by the front window.

Just as the horses reached the gate there was a brilliant flash of lightning which made everything as bright as day. We saw it was just a herd of riderless horses, perhaps frightened by the storm. It was quite a letdown. I really should have expected that, but was just not thinking. Mrs. Whitlow was really frightened and said she would not stay there alone for the world.

She was leaving the next day. Mr. Elliott had driven her to the house from Maruba and he would have taken her back to catch the train, but we thought it would be fun to walk across country to Purdy, a flag stop. It was a quarter mile. We had her suitcase and the two boys. Jimmy, of course, was used to walking; Bobby was two months younger and had never walked through the rough brushy country, and tired quickly. But we made it in time. When the train came into view, she stood in the middle of the track waving her handkerchief. It stopped and took them aboard. They were on their way to Searchlight where they would stay with Mr. Whitlow until his Searchlight duty was finished.

The September weather was beautiful. The early mornings were crisp and quite chilly when I went out to milk the cow. I had never learned to milk well, but while Bert was away I tried, and managed to get enough for Jimmy and me. One morning when I went out to milk, I found that the cow had gone through the fence out of our pasture and was with a small herd of Rock Springs Herefords.

I went out after her and fastened the rope to her collar and started to lead her home. She had always been gentle and easy to handle. But the other cattle were startled and began moving away. Foolishly, I had wrapped the rope around my wrist and when she started to follow the herd and they all began to run, I was not able to hold her. I fell and was dragged along the ground, unable to get the rope off my wrist. I was badly frightened when I saw I was headed straight for a low clump of Spanish daggers. Somehow I managed to free my hand just seconds before the loop was passing through the daggers. Those sharp, tough spears are poisonous and can make a wicked sore. I escaped with only a few bruises and abrasions. I then sold the cow to Mr. Elliott.

Chapter 11

WORKING ON THE RAILROAD

At the end of September Bert came up and helped pack our belongings to ship them to Needles. He had reserved a hotel room for the night. We arrived in Needles late in the afternoon. There was just time to have our dinner and make ourselves comfortable for the night. Next morning we were up bright and early to get started on our house.

Bert had bought a lot on the lower side of town in the poorer section. It was close to his work. He could be in bed when the ten-minute whistle blew, get up and eat his breakfast, and still be at work on time. That did not happen often, but it was possible.

I was disappointed with the location but decided to make the best of it and did not complain too much. We did not plan on staying in Needles long, and he thought by buying a cheap lot and building a small house we could save rent and have something to turn into a little cash when we were ready to go back to the ranch.

He had ordered lumber to be delivered early next morning and had asked for two days off. We had our breakfast and went down to the lot. The lumber did not get there until noon. While waiting for it, we busied ourselves getting the site ready for the foundation. We did not use a concrete foundation, but built rock pillars and set the redwood sills on those.

Billy Hutt, the elderly, genial man from whom Bert had bought the lot, was there most of the day lending a hand whenever he could. At noon the Mexican woman next door, who rented from Mr. Hutt, asked him to tell us she would be glad to have us come in for lunch. We enjoyed a meal of typical Mexican style food and appreciated her thoughtfulness. It did save us a lot of time.

That afternoon we got the floor laid and the 1" X 12" boards up around an 8' X 16' living room so we could camp there that night. Next day we got the rafters up and sheeting on the roof, but no roofing paper. Bert's two days' leave was over.

After he went to work next morning, it started to rain. Mr. Gonzales came over from next door and said that if I had a piece of canvas he would spread it on the roof. We had a big tarpaulin and it almost covered the roof. That was a life saver! It kept our furniture and us from getting wet.

Bert made amazing progress on the house considering he worked ten hours a day, six days a week, and every other Sunday on the job. He also belonged to the Santa Fe Fire Department and had to answer every alarm day or night. He received five hours pay for every night alarm, which added quite a sum to each paycheck.

When our house was finished, we had a living room with built-in wall bed, kitchen, bathroom with both tub and shower, and a wardrobe and linen closet. We built a screened porch across the entire front of the house. The inside was paneled and finished with walnut stain, the outside with rustic siding. We had good doors, casement windows, and a good, rock-lined cesspool. We planted some fast-growing willow trees in the front and back yards for shade.

Needles was a clean, attractive little desert town. There was a fine Harvey House with a well kept park beside it. Streets were paved and there was an adequate business section: a good bank (Monahan and Murphy), a J. C. Penny store, a variety store and several groceries. Claypool and Co. had both wholesale and retail grocery and general merchandise stores.

The roundhouse yard was a beautiful spot, and I guess the coolest place in town. Extensive lawns and huge shade trees made it very inviting in hot weather. We walked through it on our way to town.

The summer heat was terrific! After Bert started to work in July, there were seventeen prostrations and eleven deaths from the heat. He was one of those overcome by the heat. The doctor gave him strychnine tablets and sent him home to bed. Next day though, Bert was able to go back to work. He and Jim Noyes were living together at the time.

When Jimmy and I went down to Needles in September, the weather was getting cooler. Coming down from our mile-high ranch to an elevation of 480 feet, it was still extremely hot to me. The first two weeks I was sure I should never be able to stand the

This shot of the Santa Fe Round House in Needles
was taken several years before Bert Sharp worked
there.
National Archives Collections

heat. My whole body broke out in a heat rash. The burning and itching was agony! But after a couple of weeks It cleared up and never troubled me again.

Across the street from us lived a tall blond Englishman with a Mojave Indian wife. She was very large and dark. Their elder son, six years old, was Indian through and through. I asked him if he were going to the nearby school.

"No," he said. "Too many Messicans and Negroes."

His father had a good job with the City Power and Light Co. and drove a company truck. He took the boy up to the hilltop school every day. The younger son was blond like his father.

One morning the father came over and said to Bert, "My new son was born last night. I knew nothing about it until I heard it cry while my wife was getting breakfast this morning." She was self-sufficient to say the least.

When the men from the roundhouse came home from work, it was hard to tell whether they were white, Mexican, Negro, or Indian. There was so much smoke and coal dust, they were all just about the same color at the end of the day.

Jimmy always ran to meet his dad when he came home from work. Our pet name for Jimmy was Pooky, or Pooky-Jim. His grandmother had called him Snooks when he was tiny, and some way we had maneuvered it into Pooky. The little boy across the street would come over, calling to me, "Mrs. Sharp, here comes Pokey Jim and Pokey Jim's Pa."

Besides the Whitlows we had other friends living in Needles. Mr. and Mrs. Johnson, after proving up on their homestead, had moved to Needles to be near their son and his family. Homer was a fireman on the train. He hoped to become an engineer soon.

The United States had entered the war April 6th of that year of 1917. When the draft started we received the usual questionnaire. One question to me was, "Would you be able to support yourself and family?" My answer was yes. Bert did not in any way try to avoid going into the service, but the superintendent sent in a request for his deferment because of the important work he was doing in the shop there. The government had taken over the management of the railroads and they had to "keep 'em rolling." So we were there for the duration of the war.

Early in 1918 Bert was sent to the Santa Fe hospital in Los Angeles for surgery. I was concerned about sending him to a company hospital for fear that the care he would receive, or the doctors, might be inferior. My fears were unfounded. He never had better care in any hospital, and the surgeon, Dr. Tyrola, who performed the herniotomy, was considered one of the finest surgeons in the country. The operation was a complete success.

When Bert was released from the hospital my sister, Dora, drove him out to my father's place, where Jimmy and I were staying. The doctor warned him not to walk up any steps so my father built a gently sloping ramp up to the kitchen door for him. We stayed there a couple of weeks until he was able to move around normally.

We took Jimmy to the beach to give him his first glimpse of the ocean. It was love at first sight. He had a joyful time letting the waves roll over him as he sat in the sand at the edge of the surf. Sometimes he would lie down and roll with them. Bert was not able to go swimming, but I donned a bathing suit and Jimmy and I went in.

After returning to work in Needles, Bert's health was good. He was busy at the shop, frequently working overtime. He suggested that it would be a good time for me to take Jimmy and go for a visit with my sister in Ramsey Canyon, Arizona. I had not seen her since my marriage in 1913. Beatrice is her name but we call her Bee, for short. Bert had not been employed long enough to get passes for me over the other lines and I had to leave the Santa Fe at Ash Fork, a distance of some 150 miles or so. From there on I paid half fare. The trip over was only about 300 miles, but we changed trains four times: at Ash Fork, Phoenix, Maricopa and Tucson. I could not let them know just when I would arrive in Hereford, the nearest railroad station. The post office was there, and we were just in time to catch a ride out to Bee's place with the mail carrier.

Roy, her husband, had taken up a homestead and they live there still. They had a beautiful location, at the mouth of Ramsey Canyon, with many large live oak trees scattered over it as well as manzanitas and other shrubs and plants native to that area. After the winter snows and rains, the grass covered the countryside like wide-spreading lawns. It was good cattle country, and they were building up a nice herd of purebred Hereford cattle.

They had a baby two months old, their first child. Bee and I had such a good time. We had so much to say; there were so many things to talk about and questions to ask. Although she was four years younger than I, we had associated with the same group of young people and gone to the same parties and picnics in our girlhood days. Our interests were the same.

Time passed all too quickly and our two weeks' visit was over in no time at all, it seemed. On the return trip there were the same four changes to be made. When we boarded the last train at Ash Fork for the final lap of our journey the conductor said, "We are due in Needles at midnight. I will wake you when we get there."

"Oh, I'll be awake," I said, sure that I should not even go to sleep.

The next thing I knew he was tapping me on the shoulder, saying, "Here we are in Needles."

Bert met us at the depot and was glad to see us. As much as we had enjoyed the trip, it was still good to be home.

That was the year of the nationwide flu epidemic. Needles was hit hard. There were numerous deaths daily. Schools were turned into temporary hospitals manned by volunteers. There was but one doctor in town and he the Santa Fe doctor. He worked almost day and night.

We would see some robust looking man on the street one day and next day he would be dead. It did seem strange that the healthiest looking were the most frequent victims. We three were fortunate that it passed us by.

Bert was returned to the hospital for some minor surgery—a short stay this time. Jimmy and I stayed with my folks again.

Long-time friends John and Flora Rober, Mother Sharp, Jimmy and I were visiting Bert in his hospital room just after he was returned from surgery. He was still very weak and still slightly dazed from the anesthetic. Suddenly the building was shaking violently. The walls seemed to be going up and down in waves. The first thing that came into my mind was that the Germans were bombarding the coast. Then we realized what it was: an earthquake. Unless one has experienced an earthquake, one can't imagine the feeling of complete helplessness that one has.

Mother Sharp was looking out the window trying to find a spot where she could drop Bert out to safety. I leaned over him, took his hand and said, as calmly as possible, "Lie still. It is only an earthquake. Everything is all right."

It was quite a severe one. One patient died of a heart attack brought on by the shock. All visitors were asked to leave immediately so they could get the patients quieted down. We hated to leave Bert there, so helpless, but there was nothing else we could do.

When we returned to Needles we could see the results of a cloudburst that had occurred while we were away. Our yard was covered with mud. and debris up to the hubcaps of the car. The high water line showed on the outside of our house. It was a fraction of an inch below the floor level. We were lucky, too; in some of the houses in the higher part of town where the storm struck first, the water came up to the piano keys. As it drained off, it spread out over a flat area.

While in Los Angeles we had bought a Ford Model T Sport roadster from my brother Fred. He drove it out to Needles on his way back to Bisbee, Arizona, as Bert was still in the hospital, and left it parked in our back yard. The Ford had two bucket seats with the gas tank behind them and a small flat bed back of that for hauling luggage, which we elegantly dubbed the "tail end." Our friend, Mr. Johnson, christened the roadster "The Grasshopper," and so it was as long as we had it.

No one gave me any instruction in driving the car. The first time I took it out I drove over to Carter's grocery store. When I came out with my purchases, some one had parked directly in front of me so it was necessary for me to back out. I went in to Mr. Carter and told him I did not know how to put it in reverse. It was simple, of course, when I was shown how to do it. Later I went to the sheriff's office to see about getting a driver's license. He did not know It was required.

"There is no place in Needles where you can get one," he said. "Just go on driving. It will be all right."

The car was a blessing that summer. In the evenings we would drive up on the mesa, where there was always a breeze, and drive out into the desert until nearly midnight. By the time we returned home, we would find it cool enough that we could sleep in the screened porch where we had moved our beds for the summer.

The surrounding country was deep sand, the road just two wheel ruts. If two cars met, one had to pull off the road for the other to pass. It was no good for each one to pull out halfway. That way, all wheels being on the sand, both cars would likely get stuck. Bert always pulled out. He felt that our car, being so light and maneuverable, could more easily be brought back into the road.

The method was to drive out far enough to let the other car pass, then back up into the road over the track you had made pulling out. If he ever killed the motor, his shoulders would be black with mosquitoes before he could crank up and get started. Usually the breeze kept them off while we were driving.

Sometimes I would take Jimmy over to the hilltop school where there was a well-equipped playground. Usually there were other children playing there and he would join them. He always had fun even if he played alone.

One day a little girl was helping him go up the ladder to the top of the big slide. She asked him his name.

"Man," he said. "Man?" she asked, not sure she had heard correctly.

"Yes," he said, "I grew up." He was barely three years old.

Needles certainly had its disadvantages. It was a nice town in many ways, but the heat was something I could never learn to like. But Bert loved it and always carried fond memories of our two years there.

Chapter 12

BACK TO MARUBA

Everyone remembers November 11, 1918, at 11:00 a.m.! Suddenly, there were bells ringing, whistles blowing and people everywhere shouting and singing! The war was over. The news spread like wildfire and everyone knew it almost at once.

We began to plan on going back to the ranch. Making a living on the place was a hopeless dream from the beginning, but we kept trying.

The boys in the shop in Needles had been granted a pay raise, retroactive for several months. It meant a substantial check for Bert and we didn't want to leave until it came through. We waited until February, but no check came. We began to wonder if he would really get it. He asked for sixty-days leave and we moved back to the ranch. We felt sure the bonus would be paid by that time.

A group of three cattlemen from Arizona had come into the valley bringing a few hundred head of cattle and had turned them out on the range. They were Mr. Turner, Mr. Price and Mr. Hollimon.

Mr. and Mrs. Turner, a son, Earle, and a daughter, Verna, had moved into the Club House, which was still owned by Mrs. Jacoby. The Turners were friendly and well liked and everyone was glad to have them attend the dances and other gatherings.

Mr. Turner had leased the Jacoby well for watering his cattle; Mr. Price leased, or purchased, a place with a house and other buildings and a well five miles further down the valley; and Mr. Hollimon had moved to another part of the valley. Their watering places were not in strategic locations so their cattle could graze far enough afield. The rainfall was even then getting less and less each year, and the grass was soon eaten and trampled down over their grazing area. After three years most of them moved away, presumably back to Arizona.

Mr. Elliott was the only one who was able to make a living in Lanfair Valley. He was an exceptional man in many ways. He had been brought up on a farm in Missouri and had farmed in many locations: Mexico, Alaska and in Compton, California, and he

Millard F. Elliott shown at his orchard
in Lanfair Valley just west of Maruba.
Maud Sharp Collection

said that he thought he had found a bonanza when he moved to Maruba.

He located one mile west of Maruba. He fenced his land with a good barbed wire fence, and fenced ten acres with poultry netting to keep the rabbits out and planted a large orchard and many varieties of grapes. He could grow just about anything--tomatoes, corn, beans and other vegetables. Every year he had several acres in watermelons, which he was always able to sell at a good price. You never tasted watermelon unless you had one of his. They were famous for miles around and people came up from Needles and other distant places to buy them. His orchard thrived and soon he had peaches and grapes of the same excellent quality to sell.

He had one mare and did all his plowing and cultivating with one-horse implements. He managed to make his expenses and put a little money in the bank each year. His farming was all dry farming, which called for intense cultivation. He kept the surface loosened by going over it frequently with a spike-tooth harrow. He always carried a hoe when he went out in the orchard or field and chopped out every weed he saw.

He hauled water as every one else did. Lack of water was the number one problem with most of us. Those who were financially able to have a well drilled seemed to be acquiring land for speculation, while those who wanted to make permanent homes could not afford a well.

Bert busied himself getting the place livable again and getting some land ready to plant. After standing vacant for over two years the house needed many things done. There was much that needed cleaning.

At the end of his leave, Bert returned to work in Needles. After working six weeks longer, he came to the conclusion that he would not get the bonus and turned in his resignation.

My brother Tom came out again and stayed with Jimmy and me while Bert was gone. He drove the car and went to the dances and met most of the people and seemed to enjoy it, although he missed Bert.

We three, Tom, Jimmy and I, would sit outside in the evenings and Tom would play his mandolin and

The Reluctant Homesteader.
Alice Brownfield and Sam Zimmerman Collection

83.

sing. He also played the ukelele and the harmonica, though he had never had a music lesson. Many of the songs were those he learned with the Marines. He had enlisted in the Marine Corps at seventeen years of age, seven months before the war ended. He was discharged without ever going overseas--a great disappointment to him.

We planted watermelons. Bert had fenced about 15 acres with poultry wire. Nothing other than grain could be grown without protection from the rabbits. They damaged the grain a great deal, too, but it was planted in sufficient quantities that there was always some left to harvest.

A coyote is a gentleman in a melon patch compared to a jackrabbit. He will not touch a melon until he finds a ripe one. Then he eats an opening large enough to get his head in and then eats the entire inside of the melon, leaving just the green rind.

A rabbit, on the other hand, goes from melon to melon eating just a few bites of each one, usually not even getting through the rind. There would be dozens ruined in one night when one of the rascals managed to get through the fence.

Jimmy and I would go out every morning with a gunny sack and gather the damaged ones for the chickens and the cow. One day he had all he could carry, but I guess I was trying to overload him. He said, "Mother, if I just had a couple more hands and a tail end (referring to the back end of the roadster), maybe I could carry all you want me to!"

One morning I saw a big jackrabbit in the melon patch. I loaded the ten-gauge shotgun and went out determined to get him. He ran and when he reached the fence corner he stopped and sat up--a perfect target. I took a shot. He just ran a short distance and sat up again. I shot the second barrel with the same results. I was so provoked that I had missed, I picked up a rock and hurled it in exasperation. Imagine my surprise when he fell over, dead!

I had another interesting experience with the ten-gauge. We had trouble with hawks getting our chickens. I saw one flying around over the house and perch on a Joshua tree just outside the gate. I went out with the gun. As I approached, it flew to another tree. I tried to get closer, but it flew again. This time it dipped down to the ground and came up with a large snake dangling from its beak. I decided the hawk was the lesser of the two evils and never worried about them any more.

One day I asked Jimmy to bring in some wood for the stove.

"What if I see a snake?" he asked.

"Just keep your eyes open and if you see one, get away from it as fast as you can."

"Okay, Mother, I'll keep my headlights turned on." He must have had a premonition. He reached the wood pile, picked up an armload of wood and started back. Suddenly I heard a scream: "A snake, Mother! A snake!"

Sure enough, there was a large rattler beside the path. Bert really did not like to kill them, but when they were so close to the house, he couldn't take chances.

Homesteaders were always looking for ways to earn a little money, and while we had been in Needles, Louis Rochat and Mrs. Jacoby had built what was known as the Dagger Factory and had installed machinery for processing the Spanish daggers. There were heavy rollers used to press the juice from the long, green, sword-like blades leaving a tough, strong fiber. This was spread out in large wire trays to dry, and then shipped out to be used in making rope and twine. Experiments were being made, trying to find a way to use the juice in soap making.

The daggers were from eighteen to thirty-six inches long and grew in great profusion all over the valley. The people would cut and deliver them to the factory by the wagon load. Plants were not destroyed but were left to produce more next year. It seemed like a valuable asset to the valley.

Unfortunately, it did not prove successful and was forced to close down. All this happened while we were in Needles.

We seemed to need less cash than some. For example, we had few clothing problems. Both Bert and I had had an abundance of clothes when we moved out to the ranch. Aside from a few work clothes, we had to buy very little for several years. Men's fashions changed very little from year to year.

Some of the men wore jeans to the dances and most everywhere, but Bert liked to dress up a little.

I was adept with needle and thread and a little remodeling here and there kept mine near enough up to date that I always felt well dressed.

As for Jimmy's clothes, I could, with a yard of material, make a good looking little suit and hat that would be presentable anywhere. I was frequently complimented on my good taste in dressing him.

We needed something larger than the roadster that would carry a larger load. Bert bought a Rothweiller truck attachment for the roadster from Mr. Sidler at Ivanpah, and converted the roadster into a chain-driven one-ton truck. It worked, too. Instead of rubber tires, the rear wheels had wide iron rims as on a wagon wheel. The only trouble we ever had with it was that in deep sand there was no traction and we sometimes had a hard time getting through. But, it paid for its cost many times in the service we had from it.

We acquired another Model T somewhere and he made a satisfactory tractor of that by using an attachment built for that purpose. Jimmy asked when we were going to get an airplane. "When someone makes an attachment for a Model T," I said.

Sometimes we had severe thunderstorms with lightning flashing across the sky with a thousand tongues. The sharp clashes of thunder made me a little nervous, but I tried not to let Jimmy know it. We would stand by the window and watch while I tried to explain it the best I could. It was marvelously exciting to him and he never tired of watching.

One cloudy day we heard what we thought was rain approaching from the west. We could often hear it falling on the Joshua trees a minute or two before it reached the house. This time it did not seem to come any closer. It dawned on me that it might be that the dry wash not far from the house was running full of water. We walked over and found a raging torrent from bank to bank, fifty feet wide or more, carrying Joshua trees, railroad ties, brush and other debris rapidly down the valley. It was four to five feet deep and we could hear the boulders tumbling along the bottom. This was coming from the west, where there had been a cloudburst over the New York Mountains.

We followed the stream down about half a mile to the point where it joined another--wider, but not so deep--that came from a northwesterly direction. There was a tremendous amount of water rushing madly to the sea. If all that could have been saved for future use, just think what it could have done for that arid country!

Despite the difficulties in getting adequate water, people still tried to settle there. The McClellans and Kouschs had been friends in Los Angeles. They filed on adjacent parcels of land one mile north of Maruba, west of the tracks, building their houses near the dividing line so they were quite close together.

Mrs. McClellan had been quite ill and when they moved in, she was carried on a stretcher from the station to their house. She improved so rapidly that in a few months she was able to walk the mile to the post office.

John Kousch relinquished that claim and filed on one farther down the valley a few miles southeast of Maruba. He built a house there and moved down.

One day, after Kouschs had moved, Mrs. McClellan was at home alone when she noticed two men walking around down by Kousch's house peeking in the windows and examining everything around the place. When they came on up to her house and knocked on the door, she opened it. They asked her where those other people were. She said she did not know, but they were expected back momentarily. Then they told her to give them coffee, bacon, sugar and were going on with a list of demands. She was ready for them. She pulled her revolver out from under her apron and said, "I think it is time for you to beat it." They left and did not look back.

Mr. Ross was another neighbor and friend. His place was one mile west of Mr. Elliott's. His northeast corner joined Mr. Elliott's southwest corner. Each had filed on one half-section under the Grazing Act in addition to his homestead, giving each a full seciton. Mr. Ross had bought the Dahl property adjoining his so he owned 960 acres. He had an ice route in Alhambra in the hot summer months and the rest of the year he spent at Maruba improving his place. He had fenced it all and built a comfortable little house with a cellar. He dug a very large cistern and plastered it and built a huge barn with a sheet iron roof so he could catch the rain water in his cistern. He was a very ambitious and energetic man. Alone, he cleared and plowed a forty-foot roadway from Maruba to his place and across the west end of Mr. Elliott's place, a distance of three miles.

The road to Maruba, coming from the New York Mountains where the Giant Ledge and the Gold Chief mines were located, ran through Mr. Elliott's place and part of Mr. Ross's. It had been open to the public long enough that it had to be kept open as long as anyone wanted to use it. Mr. Ross thought that people would be glad to use a straight and better-graded road even though it was a little further to Maruba. Everyone was happy with it except George Carruthers, who lived at Giant Ledge mine. He refused to use it and insisted that the old winding road be left open. So after all that work, both Mr. Elliott and Mr. Ross had to fence along each side of the original road where it went through their places.

Chapter 13

A BUSINESS VENTURE

Bert and Mr. Elliott decided to open a small grocery and gas station. Mr. Elliott felt that so long as he had to be at the post office on train days anyway they might as well try to make a little profit. He didn't feel able to do it alone; he was past middle-age. Together they made a good team.

Bert built a counter and shelves in the post office building and added a small room at the rear for storage and a locker room outside for storing gasoline, oil and other supplies.

We arranged to have Claypool Wholesale Grocers ship the majority of our stock. Our flour, corn meal and grain were shipped from Globe Mills in Colton. The gasoline and oils were from Standard Oil in Needles. I was sworn in as Assistant Postmaster and we were ready for business. It was surprising how much we sold.

The gasoline was shipped to us in 50-gallon drums. If we failed to return an empty drum, we were billed $18 for it. We had trouble about that only once. The customers frequently purchased a full drum of gas and kept the drum until it was emptied. Standard had billed us for one and we did not know where it was. We asked everyone, but no one seemed to have it. We were quite sure where it was, but when we asked the man about it, he said he did not have it. Bert drove up there one day and there it was. He said he had forgotten about it, and raised no objection to Bert's taking it. So that was cleared up. The drums were all numbered and after that, we kept careful account of where they went.

It was interesting having all the people coming in. We got to know almost everyone in the area and looked forward to Mondays and Fridays. They were the only days we opened the store. All the homesteaders came in for their mail and most of them bought at least a portion of their supplies from us.

We would take their eggs and homemade butter and ship them to Searchlight. Both we and Mr. Elliott had chickens and had a few dozen eggs of our own to ship each week. Sugar was high. At one time it went

Pinto Valley School.
Anson Murphy Collection

90.

up to 26 cents a pound. Gasoline was 42 cents a gallon; higher than I had ever seen it. Of course, the shipping charges added considerably to the cost of everything. Our profit on gasoline was only 4 cents a gallon. We tried to keep our prices down to what they would be in Los Angeles plus freight charges.

The store was a busy place on the eight or nine days a month we opened it. We were kept up to date on all the happenings. The homesteaders made of it a sort of holiday and gossip session, discussing everything that went on around the country.

That was when we started going to the dances at the Pinto Valley Schoolhouse every other Saturday night. Now that we had the car we could get around a little more. We had such good times. No one seemed to have a care in the world. Jimmy would fall asleep on one of the benches. I would cover him and make him comfortable, and he slept until the dance was over. Sometimes, he would not awaken when we took him home, put his pajamas on and got him into bed. The moonlight nights were so bright that we often drove home without headlights. Now and then the sun would be coming up over the mountains by the time we reached home.

By this time Mr. Elliott's orchard was producing apricots, peaches and grapes in appreciable quantities. We sold some of the fruit and melons in the store. I canned the surplus peaches and made dozens of pints of Concord grape jelly. We sold peaches at 75 cents a quart and the grape jelly at 75 cents a pint. Mr. Elliott had many varieties of grapes including Black Hamburg and Thompson Seedless.

A few weeks after we opened the store, we received a check by mail from the Santa Fe in Needles for over three hundred dollars. We were puzzled. We thought it had been sent by mistake and decided the only thing to do was send it back. Later that day before the mail went out, it dawned on me that it was the check we had waited for in Needles all those months.

"This is your bonus, Bert." I said. The next week another check arrived, larger than the first. The two checks totalled more than $700. That certainly gave us a big lift.

By this time, some of the homesteaders were beginning to leave the valley. Among them were the Bells, one of the first families to have settled there. Mr. Bell, Mrs. Bell, a daughter, Nina, and son, Ed, had each filed a claim. Nina's piece joined that of her parents and her house was built just across the dividing line a few yards from theirs so they could be company for each other. They had well built, attractive little homes.

All three had proven up on their claims and were preparing to move back to their former homes in Long Beach. They sent invitations to everyone in the valley to an "at home" on a Sunday afternoon. There must have been a hundred or more guests. All were expected to stay for the evening. Supper had been prepared for everyone. There were mountains of sandwiches, salads and other foods. Mrs. Bell and Nina must have spent days preparing all that food. There were the chickens to be dressed and cooked and bread to be baked for various kinds of sandwiches. There were cakes and pies to be baked and gallons of ice cream to be made. There was a choice of coffee, lemonade or milk to drink.

The reception was a huge success. Everyone enjoyed it immensely though there was a note of sadness, too, at the thought of the family leaving the valley. They were universally liked and would be missed by many of us after they were gone.

Mother Sharp came out that summer to visit us. She had been concerned about us because she had the idea that we were just sort of camping. She was agreeably surprised when she saw that we had built a snug, comfortable little house and that it was quite livable. We did try to make a real home of it.

She seemed to have a wonderful time. I drove her around the valley and showed her some of our favorite spots. She met quite a number of the people. Mrs. Wells, over in Pinto Valley, invited us over for lunch. That made a nice trip for Mother Sharp. She saw that we had friends and neighbors and lived normal lives.

The high altitude was bad for her heart and she stayed only two weeks. But she went back home quite content about us and our way of life.

Chapter 14

DISCOURAGING DAYS

In the spring I planted a small garden; several rows of peas, radishes and onions. They were coming up nicely. The peas were about two inches high. I had followed Mr. Elliott's method of planting. I made a trench about six inches deep or until moist earth was reached and then planted and covered the seeds, not too deep. As the plants grew, I would pull the soil up around them until it was level with the top of the ground.

Shortly after my peas had sprouted, a terrific dust storm blew over the hills southwest of us. It blew all day and night. Next morning my garden was completely covered with silt. The trenches were filled up even with the top of the ground. I carefully raked the silt away from the peas. They looked none the worse and kept on growing all week.

The next week another dust storm came and repeated the process. I gave it up then and did not try to do any more with it.

When a friend from Needles, Earl Hodges, came up one Sunday, he said, "You folks ought to go up on my place in Oregon and start a ranch there."

"Don't say that unless you mean it," I said.

He and his girl friend liked to hunt quail and cottontails on our place and around the valley and frequently had lunch with us.

He had 900 acres along the Oregon coast; mountains on the east and blue Pacific on the west; a clear, cool stream running through the place and deer coming right down to the house. He painted a rosy picture. He said the first year would be the hardest. We would have to repair the buildings, build fences and get things in shape. We could raise hogs for quick money while the cattle were getting started.

"After the first year, all you would have to do would be to sit on the front porch and watch the money come in," he said.

He talked at length and was very persuasive and I was feeling low about losing my garden. We said we would think about it and talk it over.

The next week he was there again. We were

interested and told him we would drive up there and look it over and then decide.

"Oh, you can't get in there now. The road is impassable during the rainy season," he said.

That dampened our enthusiasm. That and the fact that he was expecting so much more from the place than we felt we could deliver made us decide to remain where we were. There are drawbacks everywhere as well as advantages, and we could not exchange our sunshine for all that dampness and mud.

While we had the store, we became friends with the conductor on the train. The refrigerator car came up on Fridays and when it returned to Goffs at the end of the line in the afternoon, the leftover ice was dumped on the ground. The conductor told Bert that if he wanted some ice he would pile it up on top of the car and, as he passed our place, he would push it off.

After the train passed, Bert would drive over and pick up a big tubful. We used it to make ice cream. The first time we got it we made the little one-quart freezer full three times. We ate the first two but could not quite get away with the third. The freezer was one Bert had had when he was a child.

It was against regulations to give away or sell the ice. Someone must have become jealous and started talking about it. That ended the ice for us. Someone always has to spoil a good thing!

When Bert came home from the store he would sometimes bring a special treat for Jimmy. One day he brought him just one chocolate cream.

"Here, Mother, cut this in three pieces," Jimmy said.

"It's too small to cut, Honey; Daddy brought it for you."

"Oh yes, Mother, please get a knife and cut one piece for you and one for Daddy and one for me. I'm a good 'vider-up.'"

It is so often said that an only child becomes selfish and thoughtless of others. Despite the fact that he was brought up for five years and ten months as an only child, Jimmy was then and is now the most generous person I think I have ever known.

We had filed proof of completion of work on our

The burro was a citizen of great respectability during homesteader days. This accommodating animal serves these children as the local school bus for the Pleasant View School near Rock Spring.
Susie E. Davis Collection

95.

Many of the homesteaders had school age children. Small one-room school houses were built for them. The County would typically provide materials and the homesteaders would provide the labor. These schools were frequently moved around to optimize convenience for the students. This picture shows the Cima school being moved.
Bob Ausmus Collection

claim on February 15, 1918. We did not request the patent until later. It was signed in the office of President Warren G. Harding, on March 7, 1922.

Other people were beginning to prove up on their claims also, and many were moving out of the valley. Some would have liked to stay but the going was too rough. They could not grow really profitable crops without water and there was not enough work off the ranch to keep them in funds. So, one by one the homesteads were being deserted.

School was a problem, too, for those who had school-age children. Barnwell's school had closed permanently at the end of the term in June, 1914. A school was started at Lanfair the next year. The parents were allowed some compensation for the transportation as there was no bus service. The Pinto School had a large enrollment and was open as long as we were at Maruba.

Chapter 15

OUR FAMILY GROWS

In the fall of 1920, I discovered that I was pregnant again. I did not feel too well most of the time, but we were all happy that we were to have a little sister for Jimmy. When I was making the layette, Jimmy would sit on the floor behind the sewing machine and work the treadle by hand while I sewed. He was getting as big a thrill out of it as I. He was a big help, too.

When we figured I had four more weeks to wait for the baby, Bert put me on the train at Goffs and I went down to stay with Mother and Dad in Willowbrook. Two of my brothers and two sisters also lived in Willowbrook and it was a happy homecoming. I engaged Dr. Turner, who had his own hospital in Huntington Park, a few miles from Willowbrook, and settled down to wait, not for the four weeks we had expected, but for seven weeks.

Bert and Jimmy were keeping the home fires burning at Maruba, and the time was dragging for them as well as for me. I sent them bakery goods: cinnamon rolls, doughnuts, cakes, etc., every week so they would arrive in Friday's mail. They had trouble with the ants; they would get inside the packages en route.

Charlie Martin, a nephew of Mrs. Froman, and Bert were out with their guns when they saw some ducks light on the big water hole. They bagged four of them. Mrs. Froman cooked them and sent a generous dish of duck and dumplings up to Mr. Elliott, Bert and Jimmy. It was a treat for them. Mr. Elliott always did his own cooking as he lived alone, but Bert was never interested in cooking so kept it down to the bare minimum while I was away.

At last our big day arrived! I went to the hospital early in the afternoon and in a few hours our dream came true. We had our beautiful baby girl.

Everything went along fine for the baby and me. Bert and I had chosen her name: Margaret, for his grandmother and Evelyn, for my mother.

Early next morning the nurses were scurrying around getting ready for an emergency appendectomy scheduled for 7:00 a.m. After several hours my sister, Belle, came in to see me and said that the patient was her husband, Barb. She had called Dr. Turner after midnight and when he saw Barb he said that they must get him to the hospital as soon as possible. The ambulance was late getting him there. The driver had lost his way going to their house to pick him up. Barb developed pneumonia and was in the hospital four weeks. The doctor found tuberculosis scars on his lung. Although they were healed he said Barb should either sleep outside or go to Arizona. Belle had half their front porch screened in, to make a sleeping room for him.

They had brought him home the day before I left for home. When I went over to say goodbye to him, I was sure I should never see him alive again. But he recovered completely and is hale and hearty at the age of eighty years.

I stayed with my mother and father until Peggy was four weeks old. Mother Sharp started calling her Peggy right from the beginning, so that became the name we always used. My sister Dora gave me a large clothes basket which we lined and trimmed up for a bassinet. So that it would go as baggage, my father built a box with handles for lifting, just large enough to hold the basket. Our clothes, Peggy's and mine, filled the basket. The shape of the basket left quite a big space around the bottom. We filled that space with vegetables from their garden: corn, lima beans, tomatoes, etc. Dora and her husband Sam always had such a well-kept yard and garden. They had just about everything in the line of vegetables, berries and fruits. I had enjoyed all those freshly picked fruits and vegetables so much that they wanted me to take with me as much as I could.

When we arrived at the depot, Sam bought my ticket and checked the baggage. When asked what was in the box, he answered, "Vegetables." Of course, they were not acceptable as baggage.

When he came back and told me, I said, "Sam, it is mostly clothes. We just filled in the corners with the vegetables."

When he went back and explained, the agent said, "If you say it is clothes, it's all right with me." So the things went along as baggage. It was very embarrassing for Sam. He was never one to deviate from the truth one iota. We had only a few minutes time until the train pulled out and we were homeward bound once more.

Arriving in Goffs at eight o'clock the next morning we found Bert and Jimmy waiting for us with the car. I can still see them hurrying down beside the train hand in hand. Bert had dressed Jimmy in the little pongee suit I had made for him. It brought a lump to my throat as I realized how much I had missed them.

Peggy was well and healthy, as Jimmy had always been, and we were all proud and happy with our little girl. There was on the market at that time a screened crib and playpen called The Kiddie Coop. Bert had built a homemade version for Peggy while we were away. She had a place to sleep free from flies and mosquitoes, though we were not troubled with them much on the ranch, or in Goffs, where we lived for two months.

We had planted an acre or so to wheat as an experiment to see what it would do. It grew very well and was just about ready to harvest when a hail storm struck. When it was over, most of the grain was scattered on the ground. We turned the chickens out in the field. They ate the grain as far out as it went, but did not venture out more than half way to the end of the field. The doves came in every evening by the hundreds, and they soon finished the wheat.

Early one morning I heard a commotion outside and looked out to find a coyote chasing the hens, just then he grabbed a white Leghorn and started away with her. By the time Bert got up and to the door with his gun, the coyote was out to the edge of the field just starting under the barbed wire fence. Bert's shot must have struck him about the mouth, because he dropped the hen and made for the wide open spaces. The hen looked as if the bullet had plowed a furrow across the thin flesh of her back. No bones were broken and she was soon all right again.

Mr. Elliott had planted some turnip seed on his place and persuaded Bert to plant the leftover seed on our place. He just broadcast the seed and harrowed it in on a gentle slope below the house. The soil was quite sandy and rocky in that spot, and he didn't expect much. In no time at all, it seemed, there were good sized turnips. Several of them grew to weigh five pounds each. It was hard to believe. We liked them raw and ate quite a few that way, but did not care for them cooked although they were firm and sweet, not pithy and soft as large ones usually are. We fed them to the cows and chickens.

Mr. Marvis used to stop by for a visit now and then. One day he told us that several of their horses had inadvertently been fastened in a corral over at Table Top, where they could not get any water, and had died before they were found. We felt very sad, especially when he said that Beans, one of our favorites, was among those that died.

George Carruthers, a man of middle age, was a droll character. He lived alone, as watchman at the Giant Ledge Mine, in Fourth of July Canyon. Some said he was a "remittance man" from England. He drove a little Metz roadster for everyday travel and general use, but on special occasions he sported an elegant maroon colored Pathfinder. He would take his girl friend out in it and often her mother would go along. He said he had the mother sit in the extra side seat, and as he went around the corners would speed up trying to throw her out. Of course, he was joking but he loved telling it. He was a rather likeable sort, though. Some of our picnics were held at his place, a lovely shaded canyon with plenty of fresh water. He eventually moved out. He bought and operated a hotel and restaurant at Newberry Springs about midway between Barstow and Ludlow.

Dart went to work in Brooke's Garage in Goffs, September 1, 1921, where he worked for two months. The Monday train to Searchlight had been discontinued. The mail and freight came in only once a week on Friday's train so we opened the store for business only the one day a week. While we lived in Goffs, we would drive up to Maruba early Friday mornings to help Mr. Elliott with the store, and to haul the mail and any freight from the train to the store and post office. After closing, we would drive back to Goffs.

Our first night in Goffs we were tired and sleeping soundly, when we were awakened by cats yowling and creating an awful fuss. We had brought our two cats down with us and were sure some wild animal had them.

Bert jumped out of bed and grabbed for his gun before he was fully awake. For a moment he did not realize he was in a different house and was confused. When he finally found the gun, he rushed out the kitchen door and into the yard a few steps without his shoes. The yard was full of puncture weeds, a sort of burr clover, with tough spiny burrs that would actually puncture a tire. Well, that stopped him quickly! He made quite a fuss, himself. The cats quieted down. It was only a normal cat fight, but Bert had a wretched time picking the burrs out of his feet.

The reason we were startled, I guess, was that Jimmy had been telling me about a bobcat getting Mr. Elliott's cat while I was away.

"I'll bet bobcats lay big eggs," he said. "They really do. I found a nest with some great big bobcat eggs in it over at Mr. Elliott's."

"Jimmy," I asked, "are you telling me that for the truth, or is it just a fairy story?"

"Oh, Mother, it's only a fairy tale."

The bobcat did get Mr. Elliott's cat, though--right there in his own back yard.

We had moved to Goffs to be closer to Bert's work at the garage. There was a ticket and freight agent at the depot, two hotels, Brooke's Garage and auto court and the post office. Several oldtimers, prospectors and others made their homes there.

The house we rented was three rooms in a straight row, one behind the other. That was the only place available. It did have cold running water in the kitchen in unlimited quantity, but that was its only claim to modernization. It was excellent water furnished by the Santa Fe Railroad from their deep wells.

We lived next door to the school. It was an attractive stucco building with a red tile roof and wide verandas on the west and south sides. Jimmy, then six years old, started to school and attended the two months we lived there. There were about twenty pupils. The teacher was a very nice, middle-aged woman. I invited her over for lunch one day and we

Drilling for water in Lanfair Valley during the homestead period the hard way.

Alice Brownfield and Sam Zimmerman Collection

103.

had a pleasant visit. She told me it was a relief to have children with the old familiar names--Mary, James, John--and she was happy with her work there. There were also a number of Mexican children as the track maintenance crew was made up mostly of Mexicans.

After Bert's work at the garage was done and we went back home we engaged John Kousch to drill a well on our place. We were to pay him $1.50 per foot and to furnish the casing. Half was to be paid as the work progressed and the balance on completion. Bert worked as helper on the job. John and Grace, his wife, had their meals with us on the days he worked. The Concord grape jelly I made was a great favorite with John. I never saw anyone else eat jelly as he did. He would butter a slice of bread or a hot biscuit, put it on his plate and cover it with about an inch of jelly, then eat it as he would eat a hotcake.

He was doing a splendid job on the well, drilling a good straight hole and putting the casing down as he went. They got down over two hundred feet. We were expecting to reach water at less than three hundred.

John was hotheaded and Bert was none too easygoing and the atmosphere was getting tense. They were getting on each other's nerves by that time. Bert decided to go down to Los Angeles again. He needed to earn some money to finish paying for the well. John was to continue drilling until he struck water. He went down to 225 feet.

One day he held a lighted match over the open gas tank to see how much gas he had. The resulting explosion blew up the engine as well as the gas tank. He was severely burned. He moved the rig away and never worked on the well again. In fact, he never did any more drilling after the accident. When he recovered, he started to work in a clay mine at Hart, where he remained for several years. I believe it was his own claim he was working. He shipped the clay out to Vernon, south of Los Angeles where it was used in making dishes and pottery.

Chapter 16

MARUBA VACATION

In February, 1922, we decided we would have to leave Maruba again. This time, we left our share of the store for Mr. Elliott. There was little business as the settlers were proving up on their claims and returning to their former homes, usually Long Beach or Los Angeles. There was a nice supply of staples and canned goods that Mr. Elliott could use and several outstanding accounts, of which he was able to collect a portion.

About this same time, the Cordtz, Brown, Dahl, Pinney, Johnson, Blair, and McClellan families left from the Maruba area. From Pinto Valley, the Husong, Wells, Schiershke, Gladwill, Bryant, Martin, Murphy and Dorr families left their homesteads and moved back to the various cities. In 1923, the Searchlight branch of the Santa Fe was abandoned, so Mr. Elliott gave up the post office and closed the store.

This time we moved to the town of Willowbrook instead of to Los Angeles. We drove our little Model T with the bucket seats. We put our big trunk (Bert always called it a box car) on the platform behind the gas tank. I put pillows and blankets on the gas tank where Jimmy sat between our seats and the trunk. He said several times during the trip, "Gee, Mother, I sure do have a 'counchtable' seat."

Peggy, who was seven months old, rode on my lap. Since it was a two-day trip I had fried some chickens and prepared other food to take along. We stopped at Ludlow and stayed the night with the Whitlows, who were living there at the time. We put our food together and had a banquet and a pleasant visit with them. He was station agent there. Next day we found the road through Cajon Pass had been badly washed out. In some places there was room for only one car. If two cars met, one had to back up until he came to a spot wide enough for the cars to pass each other. But we arrived at Dad's in good time with no mishaps.

We bought a lot and built a small house—three rooms with service porch and bath. The bonus money from Needles paid for the half-acre lot. My father, a building contractor, built the house. After it was finished, we were able to borrow from the bank enough to pay the cost of the entire building.

While we were building our house we stayed with Belle and Barb. Bert, being a plumber, was able to install the plumbing in a house Dad was building for them as well as another that he was building on the same street. That kept him busy and helped to repay Belle and Barb for the extra expense we made.

Since John Kousch was no longer working on our well at Maruba, and we did not know when we would be able to get someone else on the job, we made up our minds to stay in Willowbrook and try to build up a little bank account. After we were settled in our new house, Bert went to work for the Goodyear Tire and Rubber Co. and was there about a year.

Sam Peters, my sister Dora's husband, had his vacation the first two weeks in August. He and Dora wanted to go out to our place at Maruba and spend it there. Of course, they wanted me to go too, and I didn't need coaxing. Bert couldn't leave his job, so Dora, Sam, their four-year-old son, Glenn, Jimmy, Peggy and I started out laden with bedding and food enough to last the two weeks. We left bright and early in their Dodge touring car.

When we reached the summit of Cajon Pass and the end of the surfaced road, there was one chuck hole after another as we started across Victor Valley. There had been heavy rains and the road was terrible.

"We will never be able to make it over this road," Sam said. "We had better turn back." He just kept going, however, and we soon came to the end of that. The road ahead was much better, though still only an unimproved dirt road. Actually it was just two wheel ruts, evidently following a cattle trail as it wound around through the desert shrubbery.

Barstow is the halfway point between Willowbrook and our place at Maruba. We reached Newberry Springs, seventeen miles east of Barstow, just before dark and found rooms and meals at a roadside hotel. Accommodations were mediocre, but the setting was picturesque and beautiful, with green trees and a rustic swimming pool filled from a natural spring on

Zach Farmer fully rigged for travel in Lanfair Valley
in the late teens.
John Farmer Collection

the hillside making a lovely background. We started
out next morning, refreshed and rested, for the last
lap of our journey.

While passing through the hottest part near
Amboy (elevation 615 feet), we dropped into one of
the many dips in the road--the boys called them
'roller coasters'--and met, head on, another car
coming from the east. Both cars stopped, bumpers
touching, and no damage was done.

Three young men got out of the other car, their
heads bandaged. They looked as if they had been in
a wreck. They asked if we had a gun in the car.

"Yes, we always keep it handy," replied Sam.

They said they had been held up back along the
road and advised us to keep the gun ready. Their
radiator was steaming and we gave them water for it
from our meager supply. We would get water from the
Jacoby well while at the ranch. Those days it was
foolish and dangerous to start across the desert
without extra water. There were few wells. Almost all
the water used throughout that area was hauled in.
Even Ludlow, which was quite a busy settlement, had
the water shipped in Santa Fe tank cars.

We were never quite sure what those young
fellows were up to, nor how much of their story was
true, but they backed out of the road so we could
pass, then drove on westward. We proceeded on to
our place. We reached the ranch early enough to
prepare the beds and get supper over with before
dark.

Glenn and Jimmy had a wonderful time exploring
the next day. Sam and I went hunting and left Dora
there with Peggy, now a year old. I never shot a
bird in my life, but Sam provided plenty of quail and
cottontails whenever we wanted to cook them. One
day he brought in some doves and Dora made a dove
pie. Our kitchen range was still there, along with a
table, chairs, a sanitary couch and a bedspring, so
we had a comfortable camp.

We spent quite a lot of time with Mr. Elliott. It
was watermelon time and the fruit was ripe. How we
did enjoy those honey-sweet melons, luscious grapes
and Elberta peaches!

One day we packed a lunch and took Mr. Elliott
along on a drive down toward Hackberry to look at an

old mine there in the mountains. Sam was in his early forties, Mr. Elliott in his late sixties. It was amusing to watch Sam sit down and take a breather now and then, while Mr. Elliott kept up a steady pace without apparent effort. The high altitude and unaccustomed exercise were difficult for Sam. After all, he spent fifty weeks of the year at his desk at the Board of Trade in Los Angeles.

While at the ranch, Jimmy stepped on a rusty nail. We always carried a first aid kit, and I treated it the best I could. It seemed to be all right, but soon after we started home the next day he complained that it hurt. I was alarmed to find a red streak running from it up to his knee. We thought we might find a doctor at Ludlow, but Mrs. Whitlow said there was none. She suggested a soap and sugar poultice, which we applied and went on our way. The foot was sore and painful; I think the poultice irritated it. He cried and fussed all the way to Barstow. We found a doctor there who bathed it in a Creolin solution, lanced and bandaged it. Dora was astonished that Jimmy didn't even wince or cry out when the doctor cut it. After we were on the road again, he fell asleep and slept most of the afternoon.

Despite this mishap, we all enjoyed that vacation so much that we planned to go back the next year.

Chapter 17

WILLOWBROOK

As soon as we were able, we got another loan at the bank and had two more four-room houses built on our lot. We rented them furnished as soon as they were finished.

Bert was seriously considering opening his own plumbing shop. He always preferred having his own business rather than working for someone else.

He left Goodyear and rented office space on El Segundo Boulevard with an established electrician. He had a small area in the rear for supplies. He rigged up a service truck with tools, vises and pipe racks and when he had no job to go on he would keep himself busy at the shop cutting and threading pipe or making up fittings.

"If you want to have something done, take it to a busy person" has been said many times. At any rate, he soon had all the work he could handle. Besides the contracts for installations in the new buildings there was a great deal of repair work. He was always careful to do that as well as possible.

Jimmy started to school again at the Willowbrook Elementary School in September. He had a wonderful teacher, Mrs. Fahs, and made good progress all through the year. The winter passed quickly and it was soon time to start planning our next trip to Maruba. Sam's vacation, as always, was the first two weeks in August. Bert planned to go with us this time, but at the last minute, he found he simply could not make it. New buildings for which he had the plumbing contracts were nearing completion, and he had to be there to do the work. He said he and Jimmy would stay and try to get things finished up so they could come out for the second week. Jimmy was a big help on the job.

We had a time getting started. Five-year-old Glenn developed a big boil on his knee. Dora and Sam took him to the doctor the day before we planned to go. The boil was not ready to be lanced. Dr. Turner told them to bring him back the next morning. By that time it was ready. He lanced and dressed it and said, "He will be all right now. You may leave any time." They hurried home and finished packing, and we were off to a late start.

Our trip was about as usual--hot through the desert region. We packed our perishables, like butter and bacon, in cartons and wrapped them well in wool blankets and they kept in perfect condition. Our place was a mile high and much cooler so keeping food there was no problem.

When we reached Maruba it was nearly dark. We found the road from there to our ranch impassable; recent storms had washed it out. We slept in the Club House, but it was that no longer. Mrs. Jacoby had moved away and had stored some of the equipment from the old dagger factory there. The large wire trays were there and we turned them upside down and spread our bedding on them. They were not too uncomfortable, but the chipmunks and mice scurrying around in there disturbed us and we had little sleep.

Next morning we drove to Mr. Elliott's, and he suggested that we stay at his place. We put up two bedsprings, side by side, under the trees and made our beds there. It was wonderful sleeping out under the stars, so bright and seemingly so near. One night, though, it started to rain and we had to hustle to get our beds inside before they got wet.

Mr. Elliott seemed happy to have us there. Dora and I did the cooking and it gave him a little respite and a little change of diet. We spent our time driving around seeing the old mines and deserted homesteads, enjoying the melons and fruit and relaxing in the cool, refreshing atmosphere.

When we returned from our vacation, we found Dert and Jim busy, but happy. They had not been able to get out to Maruba after all. They were kept busy the entire two weeks. I was sorry I had left Jim and deprived him of the fun, but he seemed to be perfectly content as long as he was with his Dad and did not complain. They had not had to cook their own meals, but ate at the small restaurant there in Willowbrook.

When Peggy was three years old she started taking ballet lessons. She was tiny and graceful and the pet of Willowbrook. She did a little dance in an amateur contest at the local theater and won second prize.

My brother Tom and his wife, Edria, took her with them nearly everywhere they went. One day they had her at the beach. Tom took her out in the ocean. She sat on his shoulders. He watched the breakers coming and as they came even he would jump over keeping her head out of the water. Once he miscalculated and the wave broke over them. He was just sure she would be frightened and want to get out of the water. Instead, she gasped as she came up and said, "Do it again, Uncle Tom."

He loved to tell her tales, watching her face as he built up to an exciting climax. She had such expressive eyes and was living every moment of the story. Just as she would get to the point where tears were about ready to fall, he would burst out with something very funny, just to watch her instant change of expression and quick laughter.

They took her to a reunion of the Chaffee clan, Edria's people. There was quite a crowd, some from Colorado and other places.

My nephew had bought a pair of white broadcloth pants to wear at graduation. After having them cleaned he was unable to wear them and my sister asked me if I could not make a coat for Peggy of them. The material was so beautiful. I made it and used black astrakhan for collar and cuffs. It really was a lovely little coat and she wore it to this reunion. As always she was the center of attention.

"Where did you get that pretty little coat?" one guest asked her.

"Well, you know Tourist's old white pants? Mama made it out of them."

At first Tom was terribly embarrassed. But everyone was so amused and thought she had a clever mother, so he soon recovered and joined in the laughter.

After a few years, Bert was getting so much work that he badly needed a larger shop with space for a stock of materials and room to do his shop work.

He bought a lot across the street from his office and built a shop with an apartment above. We moved into the apartment and rented the house where we had lived. We had a salesroom in front and garage and large workshop in the rear. We added a line of building hardware and Sherwin Williams paints. I tended store while Bert was out at work. He was frequently able to sell the hardware and paint for the buildings where he had contracted the plumbing. It all worked together very well. We sent the laundry out and it came back finished and ready for use. I had a woman come in and clean the house thoroughly once a week. Other than that I did the housework during the times when Bert could be in the store.

As a very young man, Bert had admired the Pierce Arrow automobile that his employer drove to work every day. He resolved that some day he would have one. In 1928, he found one that suited him and that he could afford to buy. His long, long dream had come true. The delivered car was parked at the curb in front of the store. One of the Eagle Scouts, whose troop met in a building behind our shop, came in and looked all around. Seeing no strangers, he asked, "Who is here? The King of England?" It must have been an impressive looking car to prompt a comment like that. It was certainly a most comfortable one in which to ride.

With a group of relatives, we went up to the Los Angeles County Playground for a picnic that winter, 1928-1929. There were five cars. It was up in the mountains and the snow was deep and fine for sledding. My father, who was past seventy years of age, made a sled to take. He really had a wonderful time. He coasted down the slopes and trudged back up with the sled along with the youngsters. It was too cold for me. I stayed close to the fire.

On the way up, Barb was just ahead of us. He was having trouble on the grade. He would have to shift to low gear every few minutes. Bert eased the Pierce Arrow up against his bumper and we pushed him all the way up the grade without effort. I thought he would be insulted, thinking Bert was showing off. Instead, he was very grateful. He said he did not think he could have made it.

That was his unlucky day as far as car performance was concerned. On the way down, his brakes burst into flame. Again, we were following him and pulled around to flag him down. The fire was extinguished with very little damage having been done.

Chapter 18

BACK TO MARUBA AGAIN

During those years in Willowbrook we were blessed with good health and good fortune. Our work had enabled us to accumulate a little property. Always in our hearts and minds had been the longing and planning to return to Maruba. By the end of 1928, we figured we would have enough from our rentals and the sale of our business to go up there and do the things we wanted to do: finish our well, add some rooms to our house and just enjoy life. So we sold out and after a month's vacation at Clear Lake, we got our things together once more and moved back to the ranch. The children were just as eager to go as Bert and I were.

I had not done any driving since we moved to town, so I had to get a driver's license. Bert thought I would just get a temporary one so I could drive to the ranch. However, I had a perfect score in answering the questions and did not have to demonstrate my ability to drive so I was given a permanent license. At the time a license was good until revoked. It was some years later that all driver's licenses were revoked and new ones issued for a stated number of years.

Jim was just under fourteen years of age but was able to get his license, also. He was an excellent driver and able to pass all the tests.

Bert loaded our furniture on the Model T truck which he drove. Jim had a Ford roadster and I took the Pierce Arrow. Peggy rode with me. All three cars were well loaded. I had the sewing machine and a large Fada radio in the back part of the car--the Pierce had no trunk. I also carried our camping equipment.

Cajon Pass was not the well-graded, paved highway it is today but was narrow with winding grades. It had been surfaced with blacktop, though, so it was no longer muddy during rainy weather.

Bert was afraid Jim and I might have trouble making the grade so he decided that we should all stop at the foot of the pass and he would take the truck over, return and drive the roadster over, and then come back for the Pierce.

We stopped as planned and had a sandwich and a cool drink and relaxed for a few minutes. Nothing was said about Bert's driving all the cars over the grade. He must have decided we were trustworthy and capable of driving across so each of us got in his car and went on without any mishaps, although when a big Greyhound bus loomed up in the distance, I wondered if there would be room for us to pass on the narrow pavement.

Trouble did develop, however, early in the afternoon just after we passed Oro Grande, a few miles east of Victorville. The truck motor began to knock loudly. We pulled off the road into a large cleared space. Bert checked the motor and found two burned-out rods. He took them out and went to Oro Grande where he was lucky enough to find two that he could use.

We made camp for the night. We had an umbrella tent with a floor, a Coleman lantern and camp stove. I prepared our supper, and after we ate Peggy and I cleared up the dishes while Bert and Jim worked on the motor. Next morning, by the time I had breakfast ready, they were finished.

We had had breakfast and were nearly ready to start when a car drove by, turned around and came back to where we were. They had recognized the Pierce and stopped to say hello. We were surprised to see Windy Labhart and Tiny, a big six-footer from Willowbrook. They were looking for work; possibly going to Boulder City to try for work on Hoover Dam. The long depression was beginning and was to last through most of the thirties.

We were in no hurry to get started as we intended to camp another night on the road. Jim and Peggy loved to camp. In fact, we all enjoyed it. We made a leisurely trip and stopped just east of Chamness.

The sun was setting as I pulled off the highway into a likely looking camping area. That was the most beautiful sunset I have ever seen. It was not the brilliant, flaming sunset seen so frequently in the desert country, but was seen through the mist that was beginning to fall. The mountains beyond Bristol Dry Lake took on beautiful soft shades of pink, blue and mauve like a delicate pastel painting. That vision has remained with me through the years.

During the night there was light rain. We were all snug and warm in our tent. There were no motels; the word had not yet been coined. Here and there one found an auto court but they were few and far between so travelers had to carry provisions and equipment for emergencies.

We had evidently been in the western edge of a storm. As we drove eastward next morning there was evidence of a very heavy rain or cloudburst. In many places the highway was flooded with water for long stretches.

Bert and Jim had gone on ahead, leaving Peggy and me to gather up a few remaining articles and follow. They knew that they would have to do some pick and shovel work on the road between Maruba and the ranch before we could drive over the road.

They were not in sight when we came to a long lake of water spreading over the highway for 150 feet or more. I did not know how deep the water was nor what the condition of the roadway beneath would be. Often during those heavy summer rains the blacktop surfacing would be washed out leaving deep holes, especially along the edges.

I said, "Well, they evidently got through with their Fords, so we should be able to do so too."

I shifted to low gear and moved slowly, keeping as near the middle of the road as possible, and went through with no trouble at all. The Pierce never failed us at any time as long as we drove it.

It was just past noon when we reached Maruba. The two large dry washes between there and our place required a little work before we could drive across. Bert and Jim soon accomplished that and a few minutes brought us home again.

When the Santa Fe had abandoned the railroad through there, they had removed the rails but had left the ties. The settlers who were still there at the time took out the ties and used them for building barns and fences. Mr. Ross and Mr. Elliott had each built a large barn of them. We should have liked some for fencing, but there were none left.

Bert built a two-car garage with a cement floor and a pit for working on the cars. He used

The old Lanfair School
Drawing by Charley Rosenthal

117.

galvanized roof so the rainwater which was channeled into a large tank (3600 gallons) would be clean. That provided water for bathing, dishwashing and laundry most of the time.

The school at Lanfair, which Jim and Peggy attended, started soon after we arrived. It was a six and a half mile drive twice a day. Jim drove his roadster and picked up a boy at Maruba, Francis Duffy, who was also a pupil. There was no bus service so Jim was paid 15 cents a day for each one he transported; 45 cents for the three. That paid running expenses on the car. He also hauled most of the water we used for cooking and drinking. If the gas were low in the tank, as happened occasionally, he would turn around and back up one very steep bank at one of the washes, but he always managed to get home with it.

Mr. Duffy, father of the boy at Maruba, was there for his health. We stopped there to call one day and were surprised to be seated in our own rocking chairs. We had left them when we moved away, and the people who were there before the Duffys had appropriated them.

There were eight pupils in the school, two of whom were the sons of the teacher, Mrs. Riddle. She had taken that school because her husband's health required a high, dry climate. She said she had never had an easier school to teach nor received a higher salary. Our children enjoyed the school and did very well in their studies.

Highway 66 had been re-routed leaving the old road at Essex, thirteen miles west of Goffs. It passed seven miles south, bypassing Goffs. There was little travel through the once busy little place and the hotels, garage, restaurant and post office were soon closed. The mail was carried up to Lanfair and Maruba by Ed Clark or Charlie Gayle, homesteaders still living near Lanfair. Another auto court of some size had been planned at Goffs. Some of the grading had been done and trees planted, but it was abandoned when the road changed. The Santa Fe, of course, still runs through Goffs, since that is their main line from the east to the Pacific Coast.

Every time we passed through Goffs and saw the lovely little schoolhouse falling into such a state of

Old school house at Goffs, California. After many
years of decay this classic structure is being rebuilt
by private enterprise. This picture taken in 1981.

dilapidation it saddened us. The trees were dying, windows were broken and pieces of the red tile were falling off the roof. It was just crumbling away, with the help of vandals, who, for some reason, simply can't bear to see an unbroken window in a vacant building. There were simply not enough children to warrant a school. Those who were there were being transported by Santa Fe trains to Needles, 30 miles east, or to Fenner, 10 miles west.

We built an addition across the south side of the house, making a breakfast room at one end and a small bedroom for Jim at the other with a front porch between.

The breakfast room was large enough for our dining table, a built in seat on one side with a small cabinet at each end, and corner cabinets on the other side of the room. We painted it apple green as we did the kitchen. I did most of the painting. There were windows on two sides and a glass door opened on the front porch. An archway connected it to the kitchen.

I was proud of my breakfast room. We all enjoyed it so much. I kept my pretty dishes, hand-painted china, cut glass and silver on display in the cabinets and used them, too. I had never had the time to take care of them before and use them. For the most part they were wedding presents, which we had kept stored in trunks.

Jim's room was painted a light tan. Our living room walls were paneled up about four feet and we used natural burlap above that. The ceiling was regular tongue-and-groove ceiling. We finished the wood work with walnut stain.

Next, we built an addition on the north side, which gave us two bedrooms with bath between. We couldn't complete the bathroom until we were able to get another driller to finish the well. We planned to finish the bedroom walls in burlap, also.

The outside walls were 1" X 12" boards, upright. We nailed heavy tar paper over the boards and finished with rustic siding up to the casement windows and shingles above that. We stained it all with a dark brown oil stain. We dug a small cellar and rocked up the walls. It made a good storage place for our canned goods and other provisions.

All this was built of used lumber, some of which

had been left over when we moved our original house. The rest we bought from people who were abandoning their homesteads. After we painted it, it did not look so much like a jig-saw puzzle. It could not be told from new.

Mrs. Riddle and her family came up to call one day. The daughter, Prentiss Joe, exclaimed, "How liveable your house is." That was a gratifying compliment. That was our chief aim, to make a place to live.

Chapter 19

A GOOD YEAR

That winter of 1929 was one to be remembered. We had several snow storms, but one in particular kept us snowed in for a week.

Jim and Peggy were in school when the snow started falling on a Friday. By the time they were due home it was several inches deep. We never worried about them when Jim was driving; he could always manage to get home. But it was getting later than their usual time, so Bert said that he had better go and see if they were having trouble driving over the snow. He drove the Pierce down almost to Maruba, when he saw the roadster parked in the road and the children out throwing snowballs at each other. They had not seen him so he just turned around and came on back home. They were having so much fun he could not disturb them. They came along a short time later.

The snow continued to fall all night and next morning we had sixteen inches on the level ground and drifts up to 8 feet at the barn. It had drifted up against the fences and buildings and had filled the dry washes and low spots, making the road impassable. Bert and Jim had a day's work shoveling pathways to the outbuildings through the drifts.

For once we had our fill of snow cream. We would fill a bowl with soft, fluffy snow, pour over it a mixture of cream (or milk) and sugar, flavored with vanilla or whatever flavoring we favored at the moment, and mix until it was the texture of sherbet. It was a treat for the children and me, but Bert was not too fond of it.

Peggy and Jim were absent from school all the next week. The snow remained on the ground and became icy and slippery so it was impossible to drive over it. On the following Sunday, Mr. Ross managed to drive the three miles over to our place by using a shovel here and there. He wanted to go to Los Angeles on Monday and thought he could make it all right with his new pick-up truck. It was arranged that Jim and Peggy would meet him at Maruba at eight o'clock Monday morning. Jim thought that after Mr.

Ross had broken out the road with his pick-up, he could easily follow as far as the school at Lanfair.

They left Maruba at eight as planned, but there the plan had to be altered, Mr. Ross had trouble all the way. Every few minutes the truck would stall on the slippery road. Jim and Mr. Ross would get out with their shovels and clear the road so they could go a little further. It took four hours to cover the five miles to Lanfair. Of course, once the truck got through, Jim had no trouble following in the tracks. They arrived at school just at noon.

When Mr. Kousch was drilling our well, we had bought from a Mr. Woods a Fairbanks-Morse gasoline engine, a cylinder head and other small items of equipment which we planned to use for pumping water when the well was finished. This equipment was unused. The engine was in its original crate.

When we had moved to Willowbrook in 1922, Bert had buried the cylinder head and some small tools and camouflaged the spot, and when we returned in 1929 those things were intact. The engine, though, we had left in the barn loft and, of course, after seven years it had disappeared.

We felt sure we knew who had taken it and one day drove over to the ranch whose owner we suspected. Bert saw the engine still in its coat of bright red paint busy pumping water.

"I see you have a new engine," Bert said.

"Oh no," he answered, "that is the old one."

His teenage daughter, who was standing there, looked surprised and asked, "Oh, Daddy, is that the old one?" If we had not been sure before, that proved, to our satisfaction at least, that our suspicions were correct. We said nothing, however, One can't accuse a man without proof.

We wrote to Fairbanks-Morse and asked for the serial number. They had a record of the sale to Mr. Woods but did not start keeping a record of the serial numbers until the year following that sale. So we just charged it up to our carelessness in leaving it where it could be so easily stolen. As it happened, we had no occasion to use it anyway.

One day we drove up to Barnwell. The Cattle Company buildings had all burned down and the place was deserted.

Rock Springs Cattle Company had sold their California holdings to a Mr. Halsted. Their Nevada interests they sold to Rex Bell and Clara Bow. Since the railroad had been abandoned, there was no agent, no maintenance crew, no post office and no activity.

Dick Diamond still lived there with his wife and we stopped in to see them. He showed us his rock collection which he kept in his cellar. There were hundreds of specimens, which he had gathered through the years from the various mining communities where he had traveled and worked. All kinds of ores--gold, silver, copper, tungsten, molybdenum and many more. He had geodes from the nearby volcanic craters and many semi-precious stones. All were classified and neatly displayed. It was an interesting collection and one of which anyone might be proud.

Just driving around to see what changes had been made during our absence, we went to Ivanpah, six miles northwest of Barnwell, at the edge of a dry lake on the Salt Lake Railroad. It was just another old mining town with very little left. There was a general store and post office kept alive by the railway employees--maintenance crew and station agent--and a few dry farmers in the surrounding area.

Jim had some differences with his teacher, Mrs. Riddle, and was not happy about it. She had wanted him to kill a gopher snake that had come into the schoolyard. We had taught him to kill only the poisonous snakes. In that area, the rattlers were the only ones we considered dangerous. But Mrs. Riddle insisted that he kill it since he was the oldest of her pupils. He finally did, but could never quite forgive her for it.

I tried to make him understand that everyone sees things from a different viewpoint and called attention to the vast difference in the appearance of the New York Mountains as seen from our place and from Ivanpah. From our place we saw an imposing series of high needle peaks, while from Ivanpah there appeared just rounded hills. Mrs. Riddle had seen the snake as a possible danger to the children or at least a disrupting influence.

Chapter 20

FAREWELL TO MARUBA

We had been back at Maruba about eight months when the Depression began to get serious. Many people were out of work and small businesses were unable to keep going. Many were going bankrupt. Our rentals had to be reduced and payments stopped coming in from other sources. We started thinking of returning to Willowbrook. We knew we would have to go back and try to salvage what we could.

Most unwisely, we had left town before all our property was clear. There was no building going on; hence, no work for the plumber nor the electrician. Soon large numbers of people in Willowbrook, as elsewhere, were out of work or working on W.P.A. earning a bare subsistence. Many families were on relief. So just a year after we had arrived with such high hopes and plans, we moved back to town to take up the battle once more.

Jim and Peggy had had a happy year there. When I told Peggy that we had decided it was necessary for us to go back, she said, "I suppose I'll just cry all night."

It was especially hard to say goodbye to Mr. Elliott and to tell him we must leave. He would be left practically alone in the valley, and we knew it would be very lonely for him. Mr. Ross was the last of the close neighbors, and he died a short time afterward.

We were all sad at leaving, but we were still young and "Hope springs eternal in the human breast," so we were not crushed by the turn of events. We had had a wonderful, relaxing year of freedom and were all physically fit. We just knew we had to work a few more years and try to replenish our resources. The children were growing up and needed better schools. At Lanfair, only the eight grades of elementary school were included, so for that and other reasons, we never moved out there again.

Chapter 21

EPILOGUE

When we returned to Willowbrook, we traded our equity in the bungalow court we had built earlier as down payment on a large lot with a new business building and service station at the corner of Willowbrook Avenue and El Segundo Boulevard. There were four stores facing El Segundo and two facing Willowbrook, with a semi-circular store joining the two wings and facing the service station, which was right in the corner.

The whole building was vacant except the center section, which was a general merchandise store, and the service station. We liquidated the merchandise, opened up the double glass doors across the front and installed an excellent mechanic, Carl Phillips, filled our gas tanks and opened up. We were in business again.

The store on Willowbrook Avenue nearest the service station was furnished and equipped for a restaurant, and so we let Myrtle Lawrence open a restaurant there. We knew she wouldn't make any money, but it would look better to have the place occupied, and we didn't charge her any rent. She was a good cook and kept the place spotless, and it was surprising how many meals she served. When she would have a good week she would hand us a few dollars. Just having her there helped a lot.

I opened a dressmaking shop with Carl's wife, Sally, in the store on El Segundo nearest the service station. Carl painted a beautiful sign for our shop and we soon had all the work we could do. We got along fine. I did the cutting and fitting while she did beautiful work on the finishing.

We rented one store to a feed man who sold mostly poultry and rabbit feed. One we allowed to be used for church services, and one we gave to the Red Cross for a work room and distributing point for aid to the unemployed. They moved in several sewing machines, and volunteers were busy making shirts, nightgowns and other clothing to give to the needy. The federal government sent flour out in twenty-five pound sacks, I think it was, every week, and there

Mr. & Mrs. Julius D. Alexander of Pinto Valley.
Lynn Alexander Collection

were long lines on the days that was delivered. My sister Belle was a very busy worker for the Red Cross, and other members of the Congregational Church did a tremendous amount of work there.

That was a real depression and lasted through the thirties. No new businesses were starting up, so there wasn't a chance of renting any of our store buildings.

I don't know the date or even the year, for sure, but it must have been about 1932 that we had bad news of Mr. Elliott. His daughter, Hester, who lived in Vernon, just outside Los Angeles, came out and told us her father was very ill in the hospital in San Bernardino, and that he had talked a great deal about Bert.

Mr. Elliott had gone to the barn to care for his horse. It was snowing and there was a terrible wind blowing. It blew the door shut, knocking him down and breaking his leg. He lay there for several hours until George Carruthers, who was passing by, stopped in to see how he was and found him in the barn. He took Mr. Elliott to Needles to the doctor, who sent him to the hospital in San Bernardino.

We all went out to see him. He knew us but was somewhat delirious. He kept saying, "You can't trust anyone around here. There's one man you can trust. He has a grown son." He was referring to Bert.

That was the last time we saw him alive. He died just a few days later. We took Hester to the funeral in San Bernardino. Peggy stayed with her Aunt Belle. Bert drove us all out to San Bernardino and then rode the Pacific Electric, the big red cars, back to Willowbrook. Jim drove Hester, Myrtle and me on out to Maruba. Hester wanted to go to her father's ranch and get things straightened out and clean up the place. We all helped her clean and pack what she wanted to take with her. Mr. Elliott had told her to give Bert his 20-gauge shotgun.

Mr. Elliott's death was a great loss to us. With his passing, Maruba had lost some of its charm. He had a great deal of character and integrity, and we shall always remember him with much love and respect.

I have never seen a place disintegrate so swiftly as Mr. Elliott's did. The next time we went up there

Millard F. Elliott at his home west of Maruba.
Maud Sharp Collection

everything was gone but a few scraggly locust trees along the fence line north of the house, where he had planted them for a windbreak. Just a desolate piece of land was left.

We have been out many times since then, just for a day or so, and we still have the same fondness for the place where we started our lives together and spent so many happy years. Nearly all the land that was homesteaded there has reverted back to the state for taxes. We have kept ours, however, knowing that even if Bert and I never can go there to live, some day our children, or our grandchildren may realize some pleasure or profit from the land.

Maud Sharp at 94 in her home on her son's ranch
south of Sage, California. Photo taken in June 1984.

INDEX

132.

Gonzales, Mr., 72.
Greening, Jack, 38.
Greening, Kate, 37, 44.
Greening, Mr., 37.
Greening, Paul, 37, 44, 47.
Greening, Walter, 37, 44, 47.
Guirado, "the family," 58.
Guirado, Mrs. (Mary A.), 56.

Hackberry Hills (S of Maruba), 20, 108.
Halsted, Mr., 124.
Harding, President Warren G., 97.
Hart, CA, 104.
Hereford, AZ, 76.
Hinckley, Mr., 54, 56.
Hodges, Earl, 93.
Hollimon, Mr. (Bob), 80.
Hoover Dam, NV & AZ, 115.
Huntington Park, CA, 98.
Husong, "the family," 105.
Hutt, Billy, 72.

Indian Hill (a short distance S of Maruba), 35.
Ivanpah, CA, 30, 47, 86, 124.

Jacoby, Mrs. Elanor, 21, 22, 23, 54, 67, 80, 85, 111.
Jacoby Well (at Maruba), 67, 108.
Jacques, Mr. Frank, 27, 28.
Jacques, Mrs., 27.
Johnson, Mr. & Mrs., 21, 75, 78, 105.
Johnson, Homer, 21, 75.

Kessler Springs Ranch (near Cima, CA), 45.
Kousch, Grace, 21, 104.
Kousch, John, 21, 87, 104, 106, 123.
Kousch, "the family," 87.

Labhart, Windy, 115.
Lanfair, CA, 8, 10, 18, 21, 33, 34, 35, 36, 56, 97, 117, 118, 123, 125.
Lanfair, Mr. (Ernest L.), 33.
Lanfair Valley, CA, 8, 9, 17, 25, 36, 38, 80, 81, 103, 107.
Lawrence, Myrtle, 126.
Ledge, CA (earlier name for Maruba), 8, 9, 17, 20, 21, 23, 51, 52, 54.
Long Beach, CA, 92, 105.

Los Angeles, CA, 8, 10, 17, 20, 37, 50, 51, 61, 63, 67, 76, 78, 87, 104, 105, 109, 122, 128.
Ludlow, CA, 101, 105, 108, 109.
Maricopa, AZ, 76.
Martin, Charlie, 98.
Martin, "the family," 105.
Maruba, CA, 8, 9, 10, 11, 12, 18, 22, 25, 26, 36, 54, 56, 61, 66, 68, 71, 80, 81, 82, 87, 88, 97, 98, 101, 105, 106, 110, 111, 114, 116, 118, 122, 123, 125, 128, 129, 136.
Maruba Post Office, 53.
Marvis, Mr. (Ricardo), 37, 39, 40, 42, 44, 47, 48, 50, 56, 59, 60, 61, 101.
McClellan, Mrs., 87.
McClellan, "the family," 87, 105.
Mexico, 80.
Mike (?), 42, 47, 60.
Miller & Lux, 37.
Missouri, 80.
Morrow, Edria, 112.
Morrow, Fred, 63, 78.
Morrow, Maud E., 17.
Morrow, Myrtle, 63.
Morrow, Tom, 66, 67, 82, 112.
Morse, Mr., 44.
Moser, Barb, 63, 64, 99, 106, 113.
Moser, Belle, 63, 64, 99, 106, 128.
Moser, Dale, 63.
Moser, Tourist, 63, 112.
Murphy, Anson, 57, 69, 90.
Murphy, "the family," 105.
Murphy, Frank D., 9.
Nay, Mr & Mrs (Tim), 66, 68, 70,
Needles, CA, 10, 36, 50, 67, 68, 70, 72-80, 82, 85, 89, 91, 93, 106, 120, 128.
New York Mountains, 20, 25, 26, 37, 87, 88, 124.
Newberry Springs, CA, 101, 106.
Newman, Beatrice, 62, 76, 77.
Newman, Roy, 76.
Nicholson, Mr. (D.), 40, 59, 60.
Noyes, Jim, 67, 73.
Oregon, 93.
Oro Grande, CA, 115.
Overson, Gary, 45.
OX Cattle Company, 22, 62, 136.

Sharp homestead site showing remains of the small stone-lined cellar. 1984.
➤

The windmill at OX Cattle Company Headquarters at Maruba. 1984.